MACMILLAN MA

HAMLET

BY WILLIAM SHAKESPEARE

is to

JEAN R. BROOKS

with an introduction by
HAROLD BROOKS

First edition 1986

Published by
MACMILLAN EDUCATION LTD
Houndmills, Basingstoke, Hampshire RG21 2XS
and London
Companies and representatives
throughout the world

Typeset in Great Britain by
TECSET, Sutton, Surrey

Printed in Hong Kong

ISBN 0-333-37432-0 Pbk
ISBN 0-333-40226-X Pbk export

To write on *Hamlet* without Harold Jenkins's great edition at one's elbow would be absurd: my debts to it are manifold, as I am proud to acknowledge. With the growing recognition of Shakespeare's art as reaching its fulfilment on the stage, interpretations by actors have a particular value: I am grateful for the interviews readily given me by Derek Jacobi, Martin Jarvis, and Jack Shepherd. For practical help in the preparation of this book, it is a pleasure to thank Dr James Gibson, and in cutting my original draft, my husband, Professor Harold F. Brooks.

JEAN R. BROOKS

Cover illustration: *The Play Scene in Hamlet* by David Maclise, courtesy of the Royal Shakespeare Company Gallery, Stratford-upon-Avon.

CONTENTS

GENERAL EDITOR'S PREFACE

The aim of the Macmillan Master Guides is to help you to appreciate the book you are studying by providing information about it and by suggesting ways of reading and thinking about it which will lead to a fuller understanding. The section on the writer's life and background has been designed to illustrate those aspects of the writer's life which have influenced the work, and to place it in its personal and literary context. The summaries and critical commentary are of special importance in that each brief summary of the action is followed by an examination of the significant critical points. The space which might have been given to repetitive explanatory notes has been devoted to a detailed analysis of the kind of passage which might confront you in an examination. Literary criticism is concerned with both the broader aspects of the work being studied and with its detail. The ideas which meet us in reading a great work of literature, and their relevance to us today, are an essential part of our study, and our Guides look at the thought of their subject in some detail. But just as essential is the craft with which the writer has constructed his work of art, and this may be considered under several technical headings – characterisation, language, style and stagecraft, for example.

The authors of these Guides are all teachers and writers of wide experience, and they have chosen to write about books they admire and know well in the belief that they can communicate their admiration to you. But you yourself must read and know intimately the book you are studying. No one can do that for you. You should see this book as a lamppost. Use it to shed light, not to lean against. If you know your text and know what it is saying about life, and how it says it, then you will enjoy it, and there is no better way of passing an examination in literature.

JAMES GIBSON

NOTE. All line and page references are to *Hamlet* in the Arden Shakespeare series; and LN to a Long Note in that edition.

AN INTRODUCTION TO THE STUDY OF SHAKESPEARE'S PLAYS

A play as a work of art exists to the full only when performed. It must hold the audience's attention throughout the performance, and, unlike a novel, it can't be put down and taken up again. It is important to experience the play as if you are seeing it on the stage for the first time, and you should begin by reading it straight through. Shakespeare builds a play in dramatic units which divide into smaller subdivisions, or episodes, marked off by exits and entrances and lasting as long as the same actors are on stage.

The first unit provides the exposition which is designed to put the audience into the picture. In the second unit we see the forward movement of the play as one situation changes into another. The last unit in a tragedy or a tragical play will bring the catastrophe and in comedy – and some history plays – an unravelling of the complications, the *dénouement*.

The onward movement of the play from start to finish is its progressive structure. We see the chain of cause and effect (the plot) and the progressive revelation and development of character. The people, their characters and their motives drive the plot forward in a series of scenes which are carefully planned to give variety of pace and excitement. We notice fast-moving and slower-moving episodes, tension mounting and slackening, and alternate fear and hope for the characters we favour. Full-stage scenes, such as stately councils and processions or turbulent mobs, contrast with scenes of small groups of even single speakers. Each of the scenes presents a deed or event which changes the situation. In performance, entrances and exits and stage actions are physical facts, with more impact than on the page. That impact Shakespeare relied upon, and we must restore it by an effort of the imagination.

Shakespeare's language is just as diverse. Quickfire dialogue is followed by long speeches, and verse changes to prose. There is a wide range of speech – formal, colloquial, dialect, 'Mummerset' and the broken English of foreigners, for example. Songs, instrumental music, and the noise of battle, revelry and tempest, all extend the range of dramatic expression. The dramatic use of language is enhanced by skilful stagecraft, by costumes, by properties such as beds, swords and Yorick's skull, by such stage business as kneeling, embracing and giving money, and by use of such features of the stage structure as the balcony and the trapdoor.

By these means Shakespeare's people are brought vividly to life and cleverly individualised. But though they have much to tell us about human nature, we must never forget they are characters in a play, not real life. Remember, they exist to enact the play, not the play to portray *them*.

Shakespeare groups his characters so that they form a pattern, and it is useful to draw a diagram showing this. Sometimes a linking character has dealings with each group. The pattern of persons belongs to the symmetric structure of the play, and its dramatic unity is reinforced and enriched by a pattern of resemblances and contrasts; for instance, between characters, scenes, recurrent kinds of imagery, and words. It is not enough just to notice a feature that belongs to the symmetric structure, you should ask what its relevance is to the play as a whole and to the play's ideas.

These ideas and the dramatising of them in a central theme, or several related to each other, are a principal source of the dramatic unity. In order to see what themes are present and important, look, as before, for pattern. Observe the place in it of the leading character. In tragedy this will be the protagonist, in comedy heroes and heroines, together with those in conflict or contrast with them. In *Henry IV Part I*, Prince Hal is being educated for kingship and has a correct estimate of honour, while Falstaff despises honour, and Hotspur makes an idol of it. Pick out the episodes of great intensity as, for example, in *King Lear* where the theme of spiritual blindness is objectified in the blinding of Gloucester, and similarly, note the emphases given by dramatic poetry as in Prospero's 'Our revels now are ended. . .' or unforgettable utterances such as Lear's 'Is there any cause in Nature that makes these hard hearts?' Striking stage-pictures such as that of Hamlet behind the King at prayer will point to leading themes, as will all the parallels and recurrences, including those of phrase and imagery. See whether, in the play you are studying, themes known to be favourites with Shakespeare are prominent, themes such as those of order and disorder, relationships disrupted by mistakes about identity, and appearance and reality. The latter were bound to fascinate Shakespeare whose theatrical art worked by means of illusions which pointed beyond the surface of actual life to underlying truths. In looking at themes beware of attempts to make the play fit some orthodoxy a critic believes in – Freudian perhaps, or Marxist, or dogmatic Christian theology – and remember that its ideas, though they often have a bearing on ours, are Elizabethan.

Some of Shakespeare's greatness lies in the good parts he wrote for the actors. In his demands upon them, and the opportunities he provided, he bore their professional skills in mind and made use of their physical prowess, relished by a public accustomed to judge fencing and wrestling as expertly as we today judge football and tennis. As a member of the professional group of players called the Chamberlain's Men he knew each actor he was writing for. To play his women he had highly-trained boys. As paired heroines they were often contrasted, short with tall, for example, or one vivacious and enterprising, the other more conventionally feminine.

Richard Burbage, the company's leading man, was famous as a great tragic actor, and he took leading roles in seven of Shakespeare's *tragedies*. Though each of the seven has its own distinctiveness, we shall find at the centre of all of them a tragic protagonist possessing tragic greatness, not just one 'tragic flaw' but a tragic vulnerability. He will have a character which makes him unfit to cope with the tragic situations confronting him, so that his tragic errors bring down upon him tragic suffering and finally a tragic catastrophe. Normally, both the suffering and the catastrophe are far worse than he can be said to deserve, and others are engulfed in them who deserve such a fate less or not at all. Tragic terror is aroused in us because, though exceptional, he is sufficiently near to normal humankind for his fate to remind us of what can happen to human beings like ourselves, and because we see in it a combination of inexorable law and painful mystery. We recognise the principle of cause and effect where in a tragic world errors return upon those who make them, but we are also aware of the tragic disproportion between cause and effect. In a tragic world you may kick a stone and start an avalanche which will destroy you and others with you. Tragic pity is aroused in us by this disproportionate suffering, and also by all the kinds of suffering undergone by every character who has won our imaginative sympathy. Imaginative sympathy is wider than moral approval, and is felt even if suffering does seem a just and logical out-come. In addition to pity and terror we have a sense of tragic waste because catastrophe has affected so much that was great and fine. Yet we feel also a tragic exaltation. To our grief the men and women who represented those values have been destroyed, but the values themselves have been shown not to depend upon success, nor upon immunity from the worst of tragic suffering and disaster.

Comedies have been of two main kinds, or cross-bred from the two. In critical comedies the governing aim is to bring out the absurdity or irration-ality of follies and abuses, and make us laugh at them. Shakespeare's comedies often do this, but most of them belong primarily to the other kind – romantic comedy. Part of the romantic appeal is to our liking for suspense; they are dramas of averted threat, beginning in trouble and end-ing in joy. They appeal to the romantic senses of adventure and of wonder, and to complain that they are improbable is silly because the improbability, the marvellousness, is part of the pleasure. They dramatise stories of romantic love, accompanied by love doctrine – ideas and ideals of love. But they are plays in two tones, they are comic as well as romantic. There is often something to laugh at even in the love stories of the nobility and gentry, and just as there is high comedy in such incidents as the cross-purposes of the young Athenians in the wood, and Rosalind as 'Ganymede' teasing Orlando, there is always broad comedy for characters of lower rank. Even where one of the sub-plots has no effect on the main plot, it may take up a topic from it and present it in a more comic way.

What is there in the play to make us laugh or smile? We can distinguish many kinds of comedy it may employ. *Language* can amuse by its wit, or by absurdity, as in Bottom's malapropisms. Feste's nonsense-phrases, so fatuously admired by Sir Andrew, are deliberate, while his catechising of Olivia is clown-routine. Ass-headed Bottom embraced by the Fairy Queen is a *comic spectacle* combining costume and stage-business. His wanting to play every part is *comedy of character*. Phebe disdaining Silvius and in love with 'Ganymede', or Malvolio treating Olivia as though she had written him a love-letter is *comedy of situation*; the situation is laughably different from what Phebe or Malvolio supposes. A comic let-down or anticlimax can be devastating, as we see when Aragon, sure that he deserves Portia, chooses the silver casket only to find the portrait not of her but of a 'blinking idiot'. By *slapstick*, *caricature* or sheer *ridiculousness of situation*, comedy can be exaggerated into farce, which Shakespeare knows how to use on occasion. At the opposite extreme, before he averts the threat, he can carry it to the brink of tragedy, but always under control.

Dramatic irony is the result of a character or the audience anticipating an outcome which, comically or tragically, turns out very differently. Sometimes *we* foresee that it will. The speaker never foresees how ironical, looking back, the words or expectations will appear. When she says, 'A little water clears us of this deed' Lady Macbeth has no prevision of her sleep-walking words, 'Will these hands ne'er be clean?' There is irony in the way in which in all Shakespeare's tragic plays except *Richard II* comedy is found in the very heart of the tragedy. The Porter scene in *Macbeth* comes straight after Duncan's murder. In *Hamlet* and *Antony and Cleopatra* comic episodes lead into the catastrophe: the rustic Countryman brings Cleopatra the means of death, and the satirised Osric departs with Hamlet's assent to the fatal fencing match. The Porter, the Countryman and Osric are not mere 'comic relief', they contrast with the tragedy in a way that adds something to it, and affects our response.

A sense of the comic and the tragic is common ground between Shakespeare and his audience. Understandings shared with the audience are necessary to all drama. They include conventions, i.e. assumptions, contrary to what factual realism would demand, which the audience silently agrees to accept. It is, after all, by a convention, what Coleridge called a 'willing suspension of disbelief', that an actor is accepted as Hamlet. We should let a play teach us the conventions it depends on. Shakespeare's conventions allow him to take a good many liberties, and he never troubles about inconsistencies that wouldn't trouble an audience. What matters to the dramatist is the effect he creates. So long as we are responding as he would wish, Shakespeare would not care whether we could say by what means he has made us do so. But to appreciate his skill, and get a fuller understanding of his play, we have to distinguish these means, and find terms to describe them.

If you approach the Shakespeare play you are studying bearing in mind what is said to you here, then you will respond to it more fully than before. Yet like all works of artistic genius, Shakespeare's can only be analysed so far. His drama and its poetry will always have about them something 'which into words no critic can digest'.

HAROLD BROOKS

1 SHAKESPEARE'S LIFE AND THE BACKGROUND TO *HAMLET*

1.1 SHAKESPEARE'S LIFE

Though we do not know a lot about William Shakespeare's life, we know more than we know of any other Elizabethan dramatist's except Ben Jonson. He was baptised at Stratford-upon-Avon 26 April 1564, son of a well-to-do glover who became Town Bailiff (Mayor) but subsequently got into money difficulties. William, no doubt at Stratford Grammar School, learned enough Latin to read, and use in his writings, Ovid, Seneca, Plautus and Terence. He married a neighbour, Anne Hathaway (1582): they had a daughter Susannah (baptised 26 May 1583), and twins, Judith and Hamnet (baptised 2 February 1585). From then, though he may have been a schoolmaster in the country, and must have joined a company of actors, nothing is certainly known of him until 1592. By then his three *Henry VI* plays had earned him reputation as a playwright, and by 1593 he had the Earl of Southampton as a patron.

1594 sees Shakespeare acting at court as a leading member of the Chamberlain's Men, a company which had as manager James Burbage, father of Richard Burbage the great tragic actor. They had their own playhouse, the Theatre in Shoreditch, until in 1599 they built the Globe, in Southwark, from its timbers. Shakespeare had shares in the company, which from James I's accession became the King's Men. As he prospered, his purchases of Stratford properties are recorded; and during his stage career, some of his London lodgings; but the main events are his plays themselves, written, acted, and some published in authorised or unauthorised Quarto editions. Though in 1613 he collaborated with John Fletcher in *Henry VIII* and *Two Noble Kinsmen*, already in 1612 he seems to have retired to his fine Stratford house, New Place, where in 1616 he died. His plays, published and unpublished, were collected by two of his fellow-actors, in the monumental First Folio, 1623.

1.2 THE BACKGROUND TO *HAMLET*

Hamlet exists in three original texts: the Folio (F), mainly from prompt copy; a 'Good' Quarto (Q2, 1604-5) mainly from Shakespeare's manuscript, which lacked only final revision; and a 'Bad' Quarto (Q1, 1603) which Q2 was published to supersede because it had been illicitly and inaccurately put together without Shakespeare's permission. Shakespeare wrote the play not before late 1599 nor after 1600, except for adding the passage (II.ii.336-58), topical in 1601, on the child actors, competitors of his own company (see Arden edn,pp.1-13).

Shakespeare was writing for fellow-actors whose capacities he knew well. As a comic who sings, the Gravedigger fits Robert Armin, from 1599 Shakespeare's famous clown: Osric would be doubled with him. In the leading roles of Shakespearean tragic drama, Richard Burbage had been famous since *Richard III*.

Julius Caesar, written immediately before *Hamlet*, besides being a tragedy of Brutus (with Burbage in the part) was a revenge tragedy – the death and revenge of *Julius Caesar*. Revenge tragedy was a distinct species in Elizabethan drama. In a play by Thomas Kyd called *Hamlet* – which has not survived – a contemporary witness (Lodge, *Wit's Miserie*, 1596) records that a 'ghost . . . cried so miserably at the Theator like an oister wife, Hamlet revenge'. Christened by scholars the Ur-Hamlet, this play was one of Shakespeare's main sources. The other, directly or indirectly, was Belleforest's prose version of the Hamlet story. *Hamlet* begins the series of what are usually called Shakespeare's 'Great Tragedies': *Hamlet*, *Othello*, *King Lear*, and in 1606, *Macbeth*.

2 THE PLAY

2.1 THE PLAY AND YOU

Hamlet is a play for students of all ages. It is full of people asking questions. The comprehensive question the play asks is one we all have to face: how to live and act rightly as human beings in the confusing good-and-evil world we inherit at birth. The form in which Shakespeare explores the meaning of life and action is *dramatic*; the theatre itself a profound metaphor for discovering one's identity, role, and place in life. Through the ambivalent nature of revenge as a sacred duty which involves the revenger in the crime his duty impels him to punish, Shakespeare focuses questions on the painful mystery of man's dual nature, god and satyr, which are as relevant now as then. Hamlet's difference from the single-minded revenger of tradition marks him as 'the complex representative of us all'; a hero for whom life's complexities provide no black-and-white answers on 'right' action; who 'in seeking to right a wrong commits one' (Jenkins, Arden edn p. 146).

Shakespeare involves you in the maturing process which moves from simple questions – 'Am I a coward?' with simple (but wrong) answers, stock preconceptions such as 'Frailty, thy name is woman', and unrealistic ideals – 'thy commandment all alone shall live . . ./Unmix'd with baser matter' – to Hamlet's eventual acceptance of the limitations of sullied flesh and human knowledge. Yet what student would not seek, like Hamlet, to question the meaning and purpose of the mysteries he finds himself part of? In *Hamlet* Shakespeare takes you, with Hamlet, through an enactment of what it means to be a questioning human being, groping through much tragic waste, error, and some comedy, to arrive through constant reassessment at a workable pattern that makes sense of both life and play. The commentary will follow a similar method, for we can hardly separate our approach to the meaning of the play as critics, from our attempts as human beings to grapple with the mysteries of being.

4

2.2 SUMMARIES AND CRITICAL COMMENTARY

Act I, Scene i

The ghost of Denmark's late King Hamlet appears to the castle guards and
the level-headed scholar, Horatio, friend to Prince Hamlet. They determine
to tell the Prince.

Commentary
Imagine yourself in the Globe Theatre audience. The first scene rivets your
attention, through the ghost of King Hamlet which links past, present, and
future action (How?) to prepare you for the rest of the play. It introduces
you to Horatio and (by report) to young Fortinbras.

The opening challenge, 'Who's there?', sounds the key themes of
identity, disturbed order, and the questioning of appearance and reality.
Darkness, in the daylight of the theatre, is created by the words, with the
fear that a nameless something is about to happen. But the sceptic Horatio,
entering with Marcellus, relaxes the jerky dialogue into regular blank verse.

To surprise you by the apparition you expect, Shakespeare redirects
your attention to the guards telling you more, *but not too much*, of the
mystery. 'This thing' and 'this apparition' do not define *what* it was. You
settle down, with the actors, to hear a long account from Barnardo. Yet
the time is now the hour he says the ghost came. His unfinished sentence is
theatrically completed by the Ghost.

The Ghost is a riveting visual device to raise central issues. Yet some
directors, not trusting their audience's 'suspension of disbelief', banish the
Ghost from the stage to Hamlet's mind. But to define it as hallucination,
Catholic, Protestant or devil is to deny its chief purpose in the play, to be
a *'questionable* shape'. Its powerful silence both rebukes your wish to
pluck out the heart of its mystery and stimulates disturbing questions
about life's meaning. Both its silence and unconventional stage costume of
full armour would have commanded attention from an Elizabethan audience.

Experience of the Ghost in I.i is filtered to the audience largely through
Horatio, a human being confronting its terror and mystery with human
virtues – reason, learning, courage. Shakespeare's quiet, well-balanced
observer is a foil to the mercurial Hamlet. His scholarship gives him mastery
of the ritual procedure for addressing a ghost, which could not speak
unless spoken to, and credibility as a reliable witness, whose swift trans-
formation from sceptic to believer controls your response to the 'dreaded
sight'; and thematic importance – it is a student's *raison d'être* to ask
questions. Yet Horatio draws false analogy from 'the like precurse of
fear'd events' in ancient Rome: this ghost is primarily a consequence of
past events. The scholar's occasional wrong answer guides you to look
further than Horatio for meaning. But without Horatio's interpretations,
would you recognise that the Ghost 'started *like a guilty thing*/Upon a

fearful summons'? Why are you here shown the 'valiant Hamlet' you encountered in Horatio's retrospect, in a less favourable light?

We can trust Horatio on plain facts. Between the Ghost's two appearances, he explains Denmark's defence preparations. By his account, Shakespeare again ensures the apparition will catch you off guard. It extends the visual image of a 'majestical' silver-bearded soldier-king in full armour by re-creating a fittingly heroic past, 'when he th'ambitious Norway combated', vindicating rights 'well ratified by law and heraldry'. It contrasts the dead soldier-king's martial nobility with the live king in the next scene, ruling by devious diplomacy. The same principle of contrast informs Horatio's introduction of two more soldiers vital to plot and symmetric structure: old Fortinbras and young Fortinbras. The Fortinbras family prepares us for one of the major structural comparisons of the play: a son seeking vengeance for the murder of his father.

As the scene closes the bright, homely sound of the cock gets the disturbing Ghost off-stage, restores a sense of normal daily life, and indicates to the audience, by dramatic shorthand, that several hours of darkness have passed in a few minutes of daylight playing time. It signals the poetic coda in which Horatio and Marcellus set the supernatural visitor in a wider, remoter context of folklore and Christian tradition, contrasting in style and mood with the rest of the scene. For the first time we hear, from Horatio, of 'young Hamlet': 'this spirit, dumb to us, will speak to him'. So at last we will learn the Ghost's message. What, we wonder, is young Hamlet's relationship to the dead and living kings?

Act I, Scene ii

Summary
King Claudius, brother to the late King and now married to his widow Gertrude, dispatches ambassadors to avert invasion by the Norwegian Prince Fortinbras who seeks to reclaim lands lost by his father to King Hamlet. Royal permission to live abroad is granted, in Council, to Laertes (son of chief Counsellor Polonius) but refused to Hamlet. Claudius reproves Hamlet for protracted mourning. Alone, Hamlet expresses disgust at his mother's incestuous marriage. Informed of the Ghost by Horatio and the guards, he arranges to watch with them that night.

Commentary
This scene presents the opposition of 'young Hamlet' and 'the Dane'. Hamlet's mother completes his family pattern. The father/son theme is varied in Polonius and Laertes, both vital to the plot, and Claudius's diplomacy to avert invasion keeps the Fortinbras pair in mind.

Claudius's Council (1-128) has many dramatic uses. It clarifies the relationship between the two Kings and the Queen. It prepares for the irony inherent in Claudius's differing treatment of the three 'sons' – Fortinbras, and Laertes and Hamlet, with their identical requests to live abroad. You are bound to compare the young men as sons; each is linked with his father. The fathers – and one surrogate father – are contrasted too. What is the dramatic purpose of such contrasts?

The Council focuses the character of Claudius. His diplomacy appears to define him as an astute politician and efficient monarch. Yet Shakespeare compels constant reassessment of Claudius's ordered state as mere show, partly by the sub-text of motives and feelings conveyed by Claudius's style – its repetitions, paradoxes, antitheses, digressions, dislocations of syntax. The ambiguities, first glossing over his incestuous marriage, come to centre on the aloof, black-clad figure first identified by Claudius, in line 64 (why so late?) as 'my cousin Hamlet, and my son'. The stress on ambiguous relationships is reinforced by Hamlet's bitter pun (65), itself an ambiguous form.

By verbal and visual contrasts in the presentation of Hamlet's character, Shakespeare controls our response to Claudius. Hamlet's mood of intense feeling in his first extended speech (1–38), absent from Claudius's measured references to his brother's death, forces reassessment of the validity of Claudius's world, which Gertrude had asked Hamlet to join. 'Seems, madam? Nay, it is. I know not "seems"' strikes the keynote of Hamlet's character and by contrast Claudius's. Hamlet makes his 'nighted colour' typical of appearances 'that a man might *play*': role-playing is to be a recurrent theme. It is ironical that Hamlet, who scorned 'seems', is forced later to play roles which both hide and reveal truth. So is the discrepancy between Hamlet's confidence that he knows who he is ('I know not "seems"') and the audience's uncertainties about identity implanted from the beginning.

The exchange between Hamlet and Claudius begins the conflict of 'mighty opposites' which shapes the play. Here, in his refusal to acknowledge the King as his 'father', the moral victory is Hamlet's. Claudius's plausible diagnosis of Hamlet's attitude (a son's grief and resentment of his uncle's election to the throne) puts us on a false trail to give the real reason shock value. The stage convention of soliloquy invites us to share Hamlet's unspoken feelings. It explains his unsocial behaviour, and characterises him as an idealist shocked into total revulsion against life, including his own, by his mother's betrayal of the memory of a god-like father for a bestial uncle. The central comparison, 'Hyperion to a satyr', highlights the basic oppositions in human nature which Hamlet tries to keep apart (152), so that the soliloquy links the king we have just seen with the ghostly brother king Horatio is about to recall to us. Shakespeare's stagecraft places the solitary speaker, imprisoned in the circular structure of the Globe and his thoughts, between two contrasting stage images of him: the melancholy drop-out at Claudius's bright court, and the warm, natural friend of Horatio.

Shakespeare structures the natural torrent of thoughts in the soliloquy to teach us more about Hamlet than Hamlet knows. Heavy-sounding words alert us to his bitter, world-weary mood (129–34). The word 'sullied' (Q2)

which most editors see reason to accept against the Folio's 'solid', rever-
berates through the play. To 'melt' into the purity of dew (to die) re-
defines his wish to escape from Denmark as a rejection of 'sullied' human
identity. Having presented Hamlet's state, Shakespeare now moves in a
quickening, compulsive rhythm to the reason (137–53). The passage enacts
Hamlet's recoil from it by making you wait through 17 lines of obsessive
circling round 'a little month' and family relationships, for the climactic
subject and verb, 'she ... married with my uncle'. The climax forces
Hamlet to face the explicit cause of his revulsion, and you to make sense
of the jerky fragments. The soliloquy ends with a hissing of 's' sounds
(153–7) that directs the actor to spit out Hamlet's disgust. It guides us
constantly to revise our assumptions, as does the whole play.

Horatio's promised visit, coming next, evokes a glimpse of the once-
normal Hamlet – affectionate, clear-headed – forestalling distortion of him
as a neurotic 'case'. The shared memory of Hamlet's father recalls (a
constant theme) his human status: 'A was a *man*'. The style of dialogue,
appropriate as always, creates rising excitement. The human give-and-take
contrasts with the formal rhetoric of the court, the isolated torrent of
Hamlet's soliloquy, and the tense response to the supernatural. Hamlet's
close questioning of the witnesses breaks the regular line pattern without
breaking the driving rhythm. Resumption of the regular iambic pentameter
(254) points Hamlet's resolution to watch for the Ghost and his prophetic
suspicion of foul play (confided to you as an aside), leaving you keyed up
for the encounter of ghost-father and son, while in Scene iii Shakespeare
directs your interest to a more normal family meeting.

Act I, Scene iii

Summary
Laertes, about to set sail for Paris, warns his sister Ophelia against Hamlet's
courtship: Polonius forbids it.

Commentary
Scene iii focuses on the united family of Polonius – soon to be disrupted
by the divided family of Hamlet – his son Laertes, and a surprise, his
daughter Ophelia. Laertes' affectionate leave-taking keeps him in mind and
prepares for the tragic contrast of his return from France as avenger of his
dead father and mad sister. The plot-interest of Hamlet's courtship of
Ophelia and Polonius's well-meant ban on it intensifies Hamlet's isolation.
Advice given by Laertes to his sister and by Polonius to both, on how to
live in an imperfect world, compels comparison of their values with those
implied in Hamlet's soliloquy, and in two more scenes of instruction given
by 'fathers' (Claudius and the Ghost) to sons.

Shakespeare invests Ophelia from the first with pathos. Our fear for her romance has deeper cause than Polonius's ban: Hamlet has revealed to us, but not yet to Ophelia, a mind poisoned against sexual relationships by his mother's 'sullied flesh'. Ophelia's unexplained withdrawal can only strengthen his belief that 'frailty, thy name is woman'. Ophelia's constant association with flowers begins here. The family matters more, here, than individual characterisation. Ophelia's purpose in *Hamlet* is to be a dutiful daughter and innocent. Productions denying her chastity go against Laertes' warning to her to guard it, and Hamlet's tragic error in projecting his mother's sexual corruption on to the girl whose purity contrasts it.

Laertes' chief role here is to present, with Polonius, a memorable stage image of the close father/son relationship familiar to Elizabethan readers of proverbial precepts. The stereotype prepares us for the return of the son to avenge the father he loved, and for a critical response both serious and comic. The comedy is built into the situation of repeated advice, with Laertes' lordly giving of worldly wisdom punctured by his reversal into receiving it from his father. Directors who exaggerate Polonius as a pompous old buffoon, with his children inviting the audience to snigger with them behind his back, rob him of respect as a good father and counsellor. The prudent advice he gives his son implies a clear-eyed acceptance of human nature as 'a little *soil'd* i'th' working' (II.i.41) and high standards within his narrow premises.

The confidence informing their maxims for living challenges us to question the adequacy of such wisdom. The imagery, in view of sequels unforeseen by the speakers, often has ironic significance. Laertes, allowing that 'now no *soil* nor cautel doth besmirch' Hamlet's virtuous intentions, is ignorant, as his words tell us, of a Hamlet already afflicted by a sense of *sullied* flesh which will motivate his conduct. His trite comparison of Hamlet's love to a fragile violet will prove tragically applicable to his sister's wits and life. At her grave, Shakespeare makes him point the connection for us: 'from her fair and unpolluted flesh/May violets spring'. Another flower image of his, the worm in the bud, gathers resonance from the 'contagious blastments' which blight not only Ophelia (though not in the way her mentors fear) but also Hamlet and Laertes himself, corrupted into achieving his revenge by treachery. Such images, though culled from a young courtier's commonplace book, initiate an under-pattern of corruption, disease and mortality essential to the play's meaning. Further irony lies in Polonius, a caring father but a worldly judge of love, discouraging a courtship which you learn, at Ophelia's grave, the Queen would have encouraged.

The gap between simple appearance and complex reality is at the heart of the scene's irony, and is mirrored in Polonius's language patterns: tortuous digression (as at 94-7), extended metaphor, and, in admiration of his own cleverness, running a phrase to death. By his style, unconsciously comic, Shakespeare brings to attention (as in Hamlet's puns) a serious topic: the ambiguity of language, illustrating the world's complexity which is to prove Polonius's simple remedies consistently wrong.

Act I, Scene iv

Summary
The Ghost appears to Hamlet on the battlements, and beckons him away from his companions.

Commentary
Hamlet's encounter with the Ghost develops the contrast with Claudius and his world; proves Hamlet a man of courage and decision; gives dramatic shape to themes of identity, honour, and corruption; raises questions about the Ghost's nature; and leads us to expect an imminent revelation. The first brief exchanges (1–6) make us anticipate an apparition on the same lines as before. Yet the Ghost's cue brings, not the Ghost, but (off-stage) the incongruous *'flourish of trumpets, and two pieces'*. The cannon, fulfilling *different* expectations – of Claudius's promised celebration (I.ii.123–8) – keeps both Kings in mind. The echoes of the new King's revelry 'will still be in our ears when the ghost of the King he has murdered tells how he got the crown' (Arden edn,p.208,n.6).

Hamlet's exposition of the Danish 'custom', concerned with identity, reputation, and the infectious nature of corruption, raises questions of appearance and reality. If the efficient monarch of I.ii. hides a drunkard, what else is hidden? Hamlet's reflections point less to his 'tragic flaw' (see 5.2, below) than to the irony that he himself, obsessed with a 'dram of evil' – his mother's conduct – is guilty of blotting out the 'noble substance' of a pure life like Ophelia's. Convoluted syntax, demanding close attention, again contributes to the surprise of the Ghost.

The Ghost's entry, in its 'questionable shape', prompts in our minds (and still more in the Elizabethan audience) Hamlet's doubt of its nature: 'spirit of health or goblin damn'd'. That it may be a devil is suggested by Marcellus's and Horatio's caution, Hamlet's prayer for protection against evil spirits, and his questioning of it. The Ghost's beckoning promises partial enlightenment. Horatio and Marcellus, as in I.i, call attention to its duality, noting its gesture as 'courteous' even while warning Hamlet against the danger of obeying its summons. Horatio's warning seascape (69–78) and Hamlet's restless skyscape (51–6) create a sense of danger and darkness surrounding the fitful illumination of human life. But guided by love, and overcoming physical opposition from his companions, Hamlet recognises at the climax *what* he is compelled to follow: 'My fate cries out'.

In Hamlet's determined exit Shakespeare combines practical and dramatic purposes. Five economical lines, in motivating the clearance of the open stage, recall a major theme essential to the next scene, and foreshadow the interweaving pattern of human and divine purpose which Hamlet has yet to learn:

MAR. Something is rotten in the state of Denmark.
HOR. Heaven will direct it.
MAR.   Nay, let's follow him.

Act I, Scene v

Summary
The Ghost reveals to Hamlet that he was poisoned by Claudius to gain his crown and Queen, and extracts a vow of revenge. Hamlet warns his companions that he may simulate madness.

Commentary
The Ghost's dialogue with Hamlet characterises them and their relationship, completes the exposition, initiates the main action of Hamlet's revenge and focuses through it some major topics introduced earlier. Through difficulties inherent in the Ghost's command, we are encouraged to question its meaning, and prepared for Hamlet's dilemma, delay, and simulated madness.

The stillness of the two figures, in contrast to the frenzied action before, creates the Otherworld context. Shakespeare prolongs suspense by first answering our question where the Ghost comes from - Purgatory (2-20). Questions about the acceptance of a Catholic Purgatory are less relevant than what the word 'purgatorial' means even now to different faiths. First, it characterises 'Hyperion' as an ordinary human sinner. Secondly, it makes challengeable the authority of the Ghost's command. The Ghost's narration conveys necessary facts: the Queen's adultery. Claudius's murder of the King, the demand for vengeance. Each expands to a many-sided view of that human nature shared by father, son, mother, and uncle.

Shakespeare's stagecraft realises this theme. When acted, the supernatural vistor has human appearance and personality. King Hamlet's reputed nobility is confirmed by his concern for his country - its reputation (81-3), its deception about his death; and for the welfare of his wife and son: 'Taint not thy mind nor ... contrive / Against thy mother ought'. Yet the noble figure before us is balanced by the corruption described (or, as in the Royal Shakespeare Company's Ghost of 1984, also shown) of the 'smooth body' by the 'loathsome crust' of Claudius's poison. Imagery guides our developing exploration of man's nature, in a context of cosmic oppositions - god and beast, Heaven and Hell; with Denmark seen as a garden (compare I.ii.135-7) complete with creeping serpent, before and after the Fall.

The Ghost's exit leaves Hamlet without bearings. 'O all you host of heaven! O earth! What else?/And shall I couple hell?' shares with the audience Hamlet's realisation that the 'nature' (81) which demands revenge is rooted equally and inextricably in good and evil. Implied stage directions (93-5) register physical prostration. Stage business with his 'tables' could show a mind grasping at a steadying routine through a sense of helplessness in face of an almost impossible task. Shakespeare designs Hamlet's return to the normal world of his companions to make *us* lose our bearings. Uncertainty, growing throughout the act, is reinforced by contradictions.

The still gravity of the Ghost's narration gives way to irregular one-line exchanges, the 'wild and whirling words' and extreme changes of mood demonstrating Hamlet's barely-controlled hysteria, and rapid movement in all directions. Our memory of the majestic Ghost, reinforced by Hamlet's conviction 'it is an honest ghost', is undermined, literally, by the 'fellow in the cellarage' behaving in an irrational manner that would cast grave doubt on its 'honesty' for an Elizabethan audience accustomed to associate the area under the stage with Hell, and the irreverence of Hamlet's addresses with the jocular response usually accorded to the Vice (personification of evil in Tudor drama). The solemn ritual of swearing to secrecy disrupted by the underground echo vividly presents the absurdity constantly threatening to overwhelm man's efforts to create meaningful order.

Hamlet's final aside,

> The time is out of joint. O cursed spite,
> That ever I was born to set it right

alerts us to the tragic pattern set up in Act I. The practical obstacles to Hamlet's revenge are not in themselves tragic, or insuperable. Laertes, when seeking revenge, finds no difficulty in eluding Swiss guards and servile courtiers. True, Hamlet's problems are more complex. The Crown Prince has responsibilities to national as well as family honour. How should he bring the King to public vengeance without implicating the Queen, and being reputed a traitor? The testimony of an ambiguous ghost would hardly carry weight. Shakespeare has turned the conventional revenge situation into tragedy by revealing through it a man's struggle to come to terms with the co-existence of good and evil. Hamlet by the end of Act I is seen as a potential tragic hero: one whose finest virtue (reluctance to sully his idealism with murder) makes him vulnerable to tragic error in the one situation his character is unfit to cope with: the rotten court of Denmark under the rule of his ruthless antagonist Claudius.

Act II, Scene i

Summary
Polonius sets a spy on Laertes. Ophelia reports a disturbing encounter with an apparently mad Hamlet.

Commentary
Time has passed – Laertes, abroad, needs money; Hamlet has assumed his antic disposition, but not swept to his revenge. Ophelia's account of his distracted behaviour prepares for his rejection of her (III.i); when Polonius decides to inform the King, it advances the plot. His instructions to Reynaldo do not do so, but develop perspectives on honour, identity, and role-playing, and introduce the spying motif. Polonius's comic meddling in his son's life, juxtaposed with the serious results of meddling in his

daughter's, prepares for the fatal consequences of meddling in Hamlet's (III.iv).

The two parts of the scene invite us to consider the contradictions of human nature – a major theme. Polonius's tolerant picture of his son's casual indulgence in 'drabbing' is set against the reported intensity of Hamlet's silent 'perusal' of the girl he honourably loved. The affectionate if long-winded father is the Polonius familiar from I.iii. But his instructions for spying on Laertes link the family man with Claudius's world of political duplicity. Yet this view is offset by his troubled response to Ophelia's distress, his self-importance by the humility that confesses misjudgement of Hamlet's love. The audience, aware of the Ghost, recognises 'Mad for thy love?', ironically, as another misjudgement, equating Hamlet with a stage stereotype.

Ambiguities of language reinforce uncertainties about human nature. The 'sullies' and 'taints' which Polonius regards as natural to a young man set Laertes, inevitably 'soil'd' by the world that matures him, against the idealistic Hamlet 'sullied' by his mother's sexual frailty and warned by the Ghost 'taint not thy mind'. With Polonius's view of personal and family honour as allowing for drinking and drabbing set against Hamlet's god-like expectations, and Claudius's sermon on what he considers manly, natural, and reasonable, we are forced into constant reassessment of multi-faceted human nature.

Hamlet's mime and conventional stage costume of the distracted lover tell us that Hamlet is playing the *role* of madman, But what does his mime mean? There are no answers. Ophelia's report arouses compassionate interest in Hamlet's suffering, offsets the suffering his 'madness' will later cause her, and whets our curiosity to see and judge this puzzle for yourself. The stage imagery of 'putting on an act' in both parts of the scene prepares for Hamlet's experimental exploration of various roles in II.ii as a way of discovering human potential.

Act II, Scene ii

Summary

Claudius commissions Hamlet's friends, Rosencrantz and Guildenstern, to probe his condition. Ambassadors return from Norway to report success. Polonius offers to 'loose' Ophelia to Hamlet, while he and the King eavesdrop, to test his theory that thwarted love is the cause of Hamlet's madness. Hamlet sidesteps the probings of Polonius and his friends. After hearing a travelling player recite a revenge speech, he arranges for the troupe to perform a murder play to test the Ghost's honesty through Claudius's response. When alone, admiring the Player's passionate response to a fictional revenge, Hamlet reproaches himself for not acting on his real motives for revenge.

Commentary

Act I posed the question, how would Hamlet sweep to his revenge; Act II, Scene i asks why has he not done so? In the eight varied episodes of II.ii, Shakespeare's construction, like life, teaches us not to expect direct answers. These episodes are held together by their very diversity. They add up to an image of the world – noble, base, comic, tragic, ruthless, deceptive, mad, incomprehensible – where Hamlet, like every human being, has to define and achieve his purpose. The gap between resolution and achievement is here dramatised by the episodes *not* dealing with Hamlet's revenge, and the passing of time which 'transforms' him, and brings the ambassadors from Norway and his schoolfellows to court.

The main conflict is advanced only by the first and last episodes, the plans of Claudius and Hamlet to discover each other's secret. The apparent digressions that intervene contribute to theme rather than plot. Our sense of what is *not* happening is offset by a sense of court life so solidly re-assuring as to shake our confidence in the Otherworld claim for vengeance. It both allays and feeds our curiosity about Hamlet's delay until his outburst of self-reproach at the end of the scene reveals his own feelings and raises more questions.

In the first episode the King, self-styled 'father' to Hamlet, like Polonius sets spies on his son. How is your response to the two 'fathers' affected by the King's use of two schoolfellows instead of a servant? His instructions to them begin an active counter-movement which shows up Hamlet's inaction. When Claudius is offstage, dramatic impetus is sustained by the presence of his tools probing Hamlet by 'indirections'. The King's decisiveness, tact, flattery, and stepfatherly concern develop new perspectives on the efficient monarch of I.ii. But Shakespeare expects us to remember that Claudius is a usurper, and to admire only the skill with which he plays the role of King. The role of Rosencrantz and Guildenstern is to be malleable and interchangeable ciphers.

Expectation of Polonius's disclosure (II.i.117–19) at his entry is deferred while the second episode contrasts the King's success in foreign affairs with the unsolved problem of Hamlet. Claudius's ceremonious reception of the ambassadors, by illustrating a more attractive side of the Danish court than Hamlet acknowledges, warns you against total identification with his condemnation. The ambassadors' report provides a successful conclusion to the King's firm handling of aggression. It revives interest in Fortinbras, and anticipation that you will hear again of his redirected energies, since his request for 'quiet pass' through Denmark to wage war on Poland is left hanging.

The third episode, Polonius's delayed interview with Claudius, offsets the King's success in dealing with Fortinbras against his failure to pin down any truth about Hamlet. Shakespeare solves the dramatic problem of telling the King what you know already by two devices: the stage prop of Hamlet's letter to Ophelia, and the renewed comedy of Polonius's long-winded style, diverting attention from what he says to how, and whether he will ever say it all. The best of the joke is in the speaker's blind belief that his laboured rhetoric illustrates his maxim 'brevity is the soul of wit'. His long-awaited definition of true madness ('to be nothing else but mad') achieves comic irony through Hamlet's feigned madness, and tragic irony later through the real madness of Ophelia.

The letter, produced instead of Ophelia herself, is a dramatic surprise. This stage property varies the perspective on Hamlet's courtship. Shakespeare encourages us to make a different use of the evidence from Polonius: it is too complex to fit his tidy theory of love-madness, but does fit the play's major theme of duality. Conventional verse is balanced by sincere prose confession of love. The closeness of the ambiguous 'vile phrase' 'beautified' (both naturally and artifically beautiful) to 'beatified' in the context of 'the celestial and my soul's idol' hints at the complex emotions behind Hamlet's sweeping accusation of woman's deceptiveness to the innocent Ophelia in the nunnery scene - 'God hath given you one face and you make yourselves another' (III.i.144–6). Polonius's exclusive attention to the 'art' of the letter alerts you to the 'matter'.

Hamlet's encounter with Polonius satisfies our curiosity to see and judge the 'changed' Hamlet for ourselves. His quiet entry, *'reading on a book'* provides a stage image of the *thinking* man's inaction in prosecuting his revenge. The stage property also stresses the present meaninglessness of culture for Hamlet as 'Words, words, words'. By confounding expectation of Ophelia's distracted Hamlet, Shakespeare strengthens hints that Hamlet is only 'mad in craft'. The following manipulation of Polonius by Hamlet's superior verbal fencing shows that craft in action. Here Polonius suffers a comic reversal from dispenser to receiver of fatherly advice - Hamlet's! Knowing Hamlet is not the lunatic Polonius supposes, we laugh at his 'playing up' to that role before exchanging roles with his dupe.

To develop through comic treatment serious themes (appearance and reality, the duality of human nature, life as theatre) Shakespeare relies partly on Polonius as the audience's link-man, whose comic obtuseness and mistaken deductions alert you to the meaning he misses. His confiding asides (187–91, 205–6, 208–13) appeal to common human experience. Yet, knowing Hamlet's *un*common experience of the Ghost, we judge, not only laugh at, Polonius's attempt to explain the inexplicable by the stock example: 'truly in my youth I suffered much extremity for love, very near this'. Our recognition of his mistaken conclusions - 'he knew me not at first; a said I was a fishmonger'; 'Though this be madness, yet there is method in't' - points us to the sub-text of sense informing Hamlet's apparent nonsense.

Hamlet's apparently inconsequential dialogue is a natural consequence of his disgust with 'sullied flesh' here focused on Polonius, embracing sexual activity, old age, and death and a foreshadowing of his rejection of marriage to and for Ophelia in the nunnery scene. His allusion to Polonius as a fishmonger was never satisfactorily explained until Harold Jenkins showed (Arden edn,nn.on p.246, 464–6) that the fertility connotations of fishmongers' relations illuminate Hamlet's thought-sequence on mating and breeding, focused on Ophelia. His reluctance to act out the part 'nature' requires of him prompts his excessive recoil from the instinct towards life and procreation which are poisoned by his sense of corruption engendered by the noble source of life, the sun, through its contact with 'carrion' (181-6). The central issue expressed in this demonstration of Hamlet's 'antic disposition', while it fuels Polonius's theory of love-madness, is revealed to be the basic choice of accepting or rejecting the defilement of the human condition. More disturbing is the hint that Hamlet will impose his rejection on Ophelia. His warning 'Let her not walk i 'th' sun' leads, in the next episode, to an alternative image of woman's role if she is to avoid the world's taint - that of Jephtha's daughter, who died a virgin, denied life and marriage by her father. The alternatives are dramatised in the nunnery scene.

When in the next episode Rosencrantz and Guildenstern avoid Hamlet's appeals for honesty, he reverts to his tactics with Polonius, manipulating them by both role-play and word-play. Until then he gave them warm and unsuspicious welcome. Comparison of his reception of the young courtiers and the old one (whose failure to 'board' Hamlet prefigures theirs), with his reception of his other friend Horatio, illuminates the two worlds - his own and Claudius's - between which he is poised. The limited worldly values and stock assumptions by which Rosencrantz and Guildenstern interpret Hamlet's meanings as he defeats them in the game depending on *double-entendre* assign them finally to the King's world. Hamlet's abrupt ending to the game indicates his rejection of their political mode: 'Shall we to th' court? For by my fay, I cannot reason'. Rosencrantz and Guildenstern cannot imagine someone not as comfortable as they are in a world 'a little soil'd'. Hamlet's melancholy vision of beauty and nobility poisoned for him by inherent evil (293-10) elicits in them the cheap response of a dis-believing smile, and in us, irritation at their blindness.

To keep us constantly aware of the theatre metaphor is one of Shakespeare's ways of guiding our response to major themes. Here it prepares for the final episode of Act II, the arrival of the professional Players. The anticipatory discussion about them (314-64) prepares us for the importance to theme and plot of the play-within-a-play and the actors who perform it. Hamlet's catalogue of stock roles, beginning with 'He that plays the King shall be welcome' reminds you of the importance of role-playing to discovery of reality (and of one consummate Player-King); and the inadequacy of stock stage types to real-life complexity. The topic of adult actors displaced in popular esteem by child actors (a topical subject for Shakespeare's audience) exemplifies in the realm of theatre the fickle-ness of allegiance, which Hamlet has seen transferred from his god-like father to his bestial uncle. But it also foreshadows Claudius's end in Hamlet's awareness of the process of self-defeat - another major theme - implicit in the little birds of prey who 'exclaim against their own succession'. The stage business of Hamlet's hand-shaking with his untrustworthy friends is a strong contrast to the spontaneity of his welcome to the Players. His final warning to Rosencrantz and Guildenstern that he can see through their false pretences – 'I am but mad north-north-west. When the wind is southerly, I know a hawk from a handsaw' – simultaneously reminds you of his sanity, and marks his abrupt resumption of the madman's role on Polonius's entry.

Shakespeare's challenge to us to measure real-life complexity against simple stereotypes invites comparison of Hamlet's two encounters with Polonius. In between them, he has dropped the 'demented lover' part, making clear that with Polonius he *acts* the expected role. Likenesses between the two encounters stress both the stereotype and departures from it. Hamlet exhibits the same rudeness, Polonius the same reluctance to change his prepared scenario (when Hamlet anticipates his announcement of the Players) and his stock theory of Hamlet's condition: 'Still on my daughter'.

Shakespeare himself is constantly breaking his stock moulds with individual touches. The Counsellor/Father/Foolish Old Man types familiar to his audience through Classical Latin comedies studied at school, are allowed, in their descendant Polonius, a moving dignity that tempers our response to his comic traits: 'If you call me Jephtha, my lord, I have a daughter that I love passing well'. It is part of Shakespeare's wit that he makes the character you think you recognise as a stock type himself addicted to stock theatre types, such as the Distracted Lover. Shakespeare guides you to understand, before Hamlet does, his reluctance to play the role of the stock revenger of Elizabethan tragedy. Polonius's son has no such reluctance. The professional Players present the first example we have seen of the old-type stock revenger, thus bringing to a climax the interaction in Act II of 'stage' types and complex reality.

To study the function of the Player's 'Pyrrhus' speech, Harold Jenkins's long note (Arden edn,p.478) is the best companion. It leads on to Hamlet's plot against the King, motivates Hamlet's soliloquy, contrasts the Player's reaction to a fictitious calamity and Hamlet's own to a real one, and recalls in another, mythical, key many *Hamlet* motifs. In slaughtering Priam, Pyrrhus son of Achilles is, like Lucianus in the *Gonzago* play, both murderer and hero avenging his father's death – Hamlet's ultimate dual role; while Priam is another 'father slain' and 'King murdered'. The description of the mourning Queen Hecuba (498–505) contrasts with the brief mourning of Queen Gertrude (I.ii.140–56; III.ii.124–9).

The speech is the first of the inset plays, relevant to the parent play *Hamlet*, but requiring a different style to distinguish them from it. The way it is shaped, divided between the amateur actor Hamlet and the professional Player, and interrupted by the critic Polonius, is essential to its meaning. Hamlet's topic, the avenger, adds the mythical, Classical Pyrrhus to your collection of revengers (Hamlet, Fortinbras, and later Laertes) each forcing us to think of different aspects of what revenge means. To show Hamlet as the amateur actor gradually feeling his way into an unfamiliar part convinces us dramatically of the ironic discrepancy between actor and imposed role: between his complex moral nature and the simple 'hellish' revenger of the old revenge plays, blazoned in '*total gules, horridly trick'd/With blood of fathers, mothers, daughters, sons*', that he is trying on for size. As speaker of the rest, on Priam's slaying (464-93) and Hecuba's grief (498-514), the Player provokes Hamlet's soliloquy. Any production which treats him as a 'ham' ranting old-fashioned bombast ignores the need for heightened language not only to stand out from the style of *Hamlet*, but to convey the professional Player's expertise as a mirror reflecting truth (see III.ii.22).

Polonius's aesthetic criticisms, marking the three-fold division of the speech, break the dramatic illusion to remind us that we are witnessing a *performance* of a *fiction*, where the revenger stereotype is fitted to his deed. It is Polonius, not Hamlet, who observes and stops the actor's identification with his role (515-16).

During the prose dialogue (517-42) a counter-move in the plot is signalled when Hamlet commissions *The Murder of Gonzago* to be performed with an added speech which he will write. The renewed emphasis on plays and playing as means of probing mysterious purposes gives a unity to the diverse episodes of Act II that builds it up to its final climax, Hamlet's third soliloquy 'O, what a rogue and peasant slave am I!'

'Now I am alone' leads us to expect that this soliloquy, like his first, will take us into his private feelings to answer questions raised by his strange behaviour, now including his failure to sweep to his revenge. It does so by 'indirections'. Consider the place, purposes, and shaping of the soliloquy. In the first nine lines Hamlet, who in I.ii declared 'I know not "seems"', invites the audience to agree that the Player's identification with a mere 'fiction' of passion is 'monstrous'. Yet Hamlet next assumes that with *his* motive for passion the actor would find suitably magnified responses; and proceeds to reproach himself with cowardice – unjustifiably, for Shakespeare relies on your answers to Hamlet's questions (566-70) contradicting his. The third movement of his mind swings on the hinge 'Yet I' from the Player's performance in his assigned part to Hamlet's non-performance in his. You recognise, more clearly than he does, that he is trying to whip his complex nature into identification with the stage revenger Pyrrhus. The sudden contrast of tone in 'Why, what an ass am I' brings a realisation for you and Hamlet of the difference between play-acting, with histrionic 'words', and the real world where he must commit himself to action.

After the violent rush of jagged emotion, aptly rendered by correspondences in style with the Pyrrhus speech (what are they?), the soliloquy's final stage restores the regular metre, the pulse of revenge, the momentum of the main plot, and Hamlet's god-like reason – 'About, my *brains*'. He now derives from the 'monstrous' art of drama whose dual face both fascinated and repelled him, the plan to assault the King's conscience by staging a dramatic fiction 'something like the murder of my father'.

Though his aside to the Player introduced the plan, by theatrical convention you see Hamlet working it out with seeming spontaneity in his soliloquy. Its return here reawakens our questioning of the stock response to revenge as something exclusively admirable. When mirrored in Pyrrhus's 'hellish' aspect of mindless butchery, the vengeance required of Hamlet prescribes his decision to test the honesty of the Ghost who commanded it.

This final section of closely-reasoned argument (584-601) takes a reasonable audience with Hamlet, in his admission of 'melancholy' which may have deceived him, in his moral scrupulousness ('I'll have grounds/ More relative than this') and in his plan, raising hopes that he may achieve his revenge without tainting his mind. The uplift of the final couplet

> The play's the thing
> Wherein I'll catch the conscience of the King

leaves us anticipating Hamlet's dual test, of Ghost as well as King.

Act III, Scene i

Summary
Rosencrantz and Guildenstern report on Hamlet. Claudius and Polonius spy on the encounter between Hamlet and Ophelia. Hamlet's inner debate on the value of life partly motivates his treatment of Ophelia as a potential whore. Claudius, rejecting Polonius's theory of thwarted love, determines to send Hamlet abroad. Polonius plans another 'lawful espial' on Hamlet in conference with his mother.

Commentary
This scene picks up from Act II Polonius's plan to 'loose' Ophelia to Hamlet as a decoy, and Hamlet's play-scheme; thus connecting main revenge plot and Ophelia sub-plot. The soliloquy planning Hamlet's trap immediately gives place to Claudius and his tools advancing their counter-plans. Lines 1-55 point the irony of the King's encouragement of Hamlet's apparently harmless interest in putting on a play, and the 'sullied' Queen's hope that Ophelia's 'virtues' will restore a Hamlet unsettled by her 'good beauties', for the nunnery scene will prove how thoroughly Gertrude's lapse has poisoned her son's appreciation of beauty and virtue. In that scene, the play scene (III.iii) and the closet scene (III.iv) his dialogue with the one woman carries a sub-text relating to the other.

Ophelia's meditation upon a devotional book (a stage prop provided by Polonius to colour her presence) is the cue for his characteristic moralisation on 'pious action' by which 'we ... sugar o'er/The devil himself'. A platitude in Polonius's mouth, the King feels it as a 'smart ... lash' to his conscience. His aside is the first proof you have, outside the Ghost's word, of Claudius's guilt. It shows the conscience of Hamlet's too-simplified stage villain as still accessible, preparing us for the sequels of his flight from the *Gonzago* play and his attempt to repent.

On Hamlet's entry Shakespeare prolongs our suspense for his meeting with Ophelia while he speaks his not unrelated but much misinterpreted soliloquy, 'To be or not to be'. Some views of 'the question' have been: (1) Is life worth living or not? (2) Is it better to endure, or end it by suicide? (3) If the 'question' is personal rather than general, is it whether Hamlet should (a) kill himself, (b) kill the King, or (c) both? For critics of the calibre of Harold Jenkins, its form - the debate - demands general rather than personal application. Hamlet speaks of what *all* 'flesh' is heir to, balancing the pros and cons of life's value. The second, amplified, stage of the argument (57-60) offers in the metaphor 'take arms against a sea of troubles' a true equivalent of 'not to be' when futile opposition to an over-whelming natural force is seen to end our troubles by ending our lives. The further development of the debate depends on a series of hooks and eyes: the attractiveness of dying (60-4) followed swiftly by the objection to it that 'must give us pause'; the endurance of many troubles opposed by ease of escape through 'a bare bodkin'. Suicide is introduced only to be dismissed. The conclusion to the debate opts for life: yet not from choice but from fear of the 'dreams' that may come in the after-life. 'Conscience does make cowards of us all' concludes the question in a paradox that recognises the dual face man has to live with. The Pyrrhus qualities apparently required of a revenger call for pondering, by Hamlet and the audience, on the value of life, when to do good involves doing evil. Uncertainty about the after-life adds to the doubt whether man's cosmic context can be trusted. *Is* Hamlet 'prompted to . . . revenge by heaven and hell'?

This fourth soliloquy owes its one-sided view of life as unrelieved trouble to Hamlet's character and dramatic predicament. The immediate consequence is the nunnery scene, which translates his longing to escape life's defilement from inner debate into dramatic plot, through his rejection of marriage and breeding. His obsession with life's evils is vividly dramatised in his projection of his mother's guilt on to the innocent Ophelia. The nunnery scene also furthers the plot. Hamlet's rejection of Ophelia ends hope of fulfilment of their love, and begins the distress that pushes Ophelia towards madness and death. The Ophelia and main plots intertwine when Hamlet recalls his duty to revenge (149-50), and Claudius, alive to Hamlet's threat in 'all but one shall live', quickly determines 'He shall with speed to England'.

Anxious to find some simple real-life motivation for Hamlet's insulting rejection of Ophelia, some critics have postulated stage business revealing the spies. Others, ignoring Shakespeare's care to warn you against Polonian stock deductions, make him resentful of his recent repulse. But instead of a Hamlet resentful of Ophelia's betrayal, their expected roles are reversed. The girl who denied Hamlet access implies reproach for *his* absence 'this many a day'. The love-gifts she returns picture *his* repudiation of *her* love: 'I never gave you aught'. Renunciation of Ophelia is the climax of Hamlet's rejection of good because of the evil inseparable from it. He greets her with a reference to his own sins, not hers (89-90). He does not accuse her of betraying him – yet; he implies that because she is a woman, like his mother, she inevitably will, unless to avoid being a 'breeder of sinners' she escapes to a nunnery. After the personal 'thee' Hamlet's move to the generalising 'your' ('I have heard of your paintings', 144) while still addressing the unpainted girl you see, shows he is making Ophelia a scapegoat for woman's collective sins.

Shakespeare links the nunnery scene to others reflecting his design of life-experience. Hamlet's 'I lov'd Ophelia' – said over her grave – makes the belated commitment to love denied in the nunnery scene. The cloisters which protect from the sun follow up the former imagery in the fish-monger episode (II.ii.174–86) of 'maggots in a dead dog' perpetuated by exposure to the sun. Here, Hamlet's self-disgust transforms the 'carrion' good for kissing into Ophelia, fit to breed more vile forms of life. In both scenes Hamlet's obsession with transmission of sin from parent to child makes us simultaneously aware of father and daughter. 'Where's your father?' is an association like 'Have you a daughter?' Ophelia the virgin until death is contrasted with Gertrude the adulterous wife; the marriage that will not take place with the second marriage that should not have taken place. Ophelia's lament (152–63) points the contrast between Hamlet past and present, preparing for his return to normality in the final scene of the play.

The emergence of the eavesdroppers, with the King's shrewd diagnosis of a soul-sickness spelling danger, precipitates two plans: the King's, to remove the danger by hastening Hamlet's departure for England, and Polonius's second 'espial' to be arranged in the Queen's closet where Hamlet may confide in his mother.

Act III, Scene ii

Summary

Hamlet alerts Horatio to observe the King. The playing of *The Murder of Gonzago*, during which Hamlet insults Ophelia, the Queen, and the King, catches the King's conscience and drives him from the room. Hamlet is summoned to the Queen's closet.

Commentary

This scene swings attention from the King's plot against Hamlet to Hamlet's against the King. But Shakespeare delays performance of *The Murder of Gonzago* by Hamlet's advice to the Players and praise of Horatio. In good acting and a good man he admires a balance of 'blood and judgement', which he is here exhibiting himself. Hamlet's advice to the Players exists to give Shakespeare's advice to the audience. Distinguished from the groundlings capable only of appreciating 'inexplicable dumb-shows', you, the 'judicious' spectator, are alerted to find Shakespeare's dumb-show explicable. Actors, Hamlet advises, should 'hold ... the mirror up to nature'.

Hamlet's generous appreciation of his true friend (53-74), in steady blank verse, has a normality that brings relief from the tension mounting towards the play scene. What truth is there in the criticism that Hamlet admires Horatio for being what he himself is not? The man 'that is not passion's slave' calls up for contrast Pyrrhus rather than Hamlet. The ceremonial arrival of King and court recalls the previous public occasion (I.ii) with the same melancholy figure disturbing the harmony. But Shakespeare has guided us towards reassessment of where the disturbance lies.

The placing of this central scene between the nunnery scene (III.i) and the closet scene (III.iv) alerts you to the complex cross-currents merging Ophelia and Gertrude in Hamlet's mind. His mother's 'sit by me' elicits 'No, good mother, here's metal more attractive'. Though his practical reason for refusing a seat by his mother is to watch the King, he is ironically taking up the true-lover pose at Ophelia's feet, insulting her with a stream of sexual jests, watching with her a stage image of his mother's guilty love which poisoned his response to the young girl's innocent love.

The dumb-show focuses 'at the centre of the drama a perfect image of the crime which is the foundation of its plot' (Arden edn,LN III.ii.133, p.501). The problem it has posed for literal-minded critics and directors - why does Claudius apparently remain unmoved by this mimed preview of his crime? - will be discussed below, in 6.1, 'Problems and non-problems'. As the *Murder of Gonzago* will be interrupted, this preview of it, complete, reveals beforehand how the enacted story is designed to trap Claudius's conscience, so that we can concentrate chiefly on the watchers' response.

The purposes of both dumb-show and inset play are served by their 'old-fashioned' style. Like the Pyrrhus speech, the artificial style of *The Murder of Gonzago* distinguishes between the immediate dramatic illusion - *Hamlet* - and the illusion at second-hand. But whereas the outlandish diction of the Pyrrhus speech held a distorting mirror up to the brutal 'nature' of the revenger, the jog-trot couplets of *The Murder of Gonzago* furnish an unobtrusive background to the acute dramatic tensions. Yet in watching the silent struggle between Hamlet and the King, we must still attend to the inset play, and not only the climax '*Pours the poison in the sleeper's ears*'. An important purpose of the debate between Player-King and Player-Queen is to point parallels in the play scene to Shakespeare's total design.

Hamlet's prose interruptions, 'as good as a chorus' (240), alert you to parallels. Ophelia's 'belike this show imports the argument' (gist) denotes that though dumb-shows usually did not, this one does. Hamlet's enigmatic 'It means mischief' (135) leaves us keyed up for a meaning that is more than a simple proof of Claudius's guilt. At '*None wed the second but who kill'd the first*', Hamlet's aside 'That's wormwood' (1976) may indicate not that he suspects his mother of complicity in the murder, but some 'blenching' from Gertrude that her husband does not show - a pointer to the conscience Hamlet stirs in her in III.iv.

Shakespeare works up suspense by switching the focus from Queen to King and finally to the taunting Hamlet. The King's question whether, judging by the 'argument', the play is indeed free of 'offence', may be accepted by the stage audience as provoked legitimately enough by the insult to his Queen. But it will excite the Globe audience as his first groping towards *their* awareness that he too is the target; an awareness that must become complete with Hamlet's loaded reference, in reply, to 'poison in jest'. Hamlet's sarcastic extension of innocence to the King ('*Our* withers are unwrung') prepares for the symbolic merging of Hamlet and Claudius as carriers of human guilt in Lucianus, who enters the inset play at this fraught point. Hamlet's identification with Lucianus as '*nephew* to the King' instead of 'brother' links the re-enactment of a past with the threat of a future crime. The merged reflections of Claudius the murderer and Hamlet the revenger make Lucianus a 'mirror' of the evil in both, and of Hamlet with evil inseparable from his good; one who in avenging one crime commits another. Lucianus's speech (249-54) sustains the dominant image pattern of '*wholesome life*' '*blasted*' by poison that '*usurps*' it. '*Thoughts black*' match the internal darkness of the King who cries for 'Lights' to light his guilt-stricken departure.

The dramatic climax, 'The King rises', frustrates as much as it fulfils expectation. Hamlet's forestalling of the rest of the inset play - 'You shall see anon how the murderer gets the love of Gonzago's wife' - keeps the King's secret unknown to the court but reveals Hamlet's to him, giving him justification for exiling Hamlet as a dangerous madman.

Hamlet's dialogues with Horatio (269-88), Rosencrantz and Guildenstern (289-363), and Polonius (364-77), besides reinforcing imagery of disease and contagion (292-9, 312, 380-1), the trap and the hunt (265-6, 337-8), show the immediate effects of the play-device on his relationships. In the consultation promised in III.ii.86-7, the measured concurrence of the rational Horatio with Hamlet's elated perceptions leads us to expect some furtherance of the revenge action. But the entry of the King's tools revives expectation of a counterplot.

Rosencrantz and Guildenstern return the audience's attention to suspended threads of the plot. The King's reported 'choler' prepares us for confirmation of his plan to send Hamlet to England, and the Queen's 'affliction of spirit' for Hamlet afflicting it further in III.iv. The Queen's expected summons will set up Polonius's plan of 'espial'. Hamlet's dropping of the 'antic' mask to ask why they behave as if they 'would drive [him] into a toil', places them decisively with the King, and himself as exposer and controller of traps. His musical parable, through the stage-business with the recorder (341-63), reduces them to amateurs who 'cannot play' upon him.

Hamlet's short exchange with Polonius repeats in a comic key the serious motifs of the preceding dialogue. In the 'cloud' business Polonius would seem to know Hamlet's 'stops'; but is made to pipe to Hamlet's tune (Arden edn,LN. III.ii.367-73), p.510). Polonius's ready agreement with Hamlet's contradictory definitions comments on Hamlet's warning against attempts to 'pluck out the heart of [his] mystery' (354-63), and the changeable appearances of reality. Polonius as messenger from the Queen connects this scene with the next two. Hamlet's cat-and-mouse game with all the King's tools, though the audience enjoys it, accords by its streak of cruelty with his treatment of Ophelia, and the hellish side of man's nature released by the play scene, reinforced in the following soliloquy.

Hamlet's fifth soliloquy (379-90) shows a vindictive glorying in blood-lust. Its form, a condensed version of the conventional 'night-piece' in revenge tragedy prefacing a deed of blood, uses stock imagery in the first five lines to link this Hamlet to the play's doers of evil – 'hellish' Pyrrhus; Lucianus with his witches' brew 'of midnight weeds'; and Claudius, whose 'bitter business' spread 'contagion' through his kingdom. Do we want Hamlet to accomplish his revenge in a devilish spirit? The Ghost, recalled by 'When churchyards yawn', did not ('Taint not thy mind'). 'Soft, now to my mother' resumes movement in the plot and in Hamlet, from the two-dimensional stock villain back to the conflicting demands of his dual nature. When Hamlet lets loose the evil in it, some actors and critics revolt. But to assume that he does not mean what he says ignores the central position of this speech, preluding the two most important consequences of Hamlet's 'hellish' phase which bring the rising action to a climax: his failure to kill the King and the killing of Polonius.

Act III, Scene iii

Summary

Claudius, fearing retribution, orders Rosencrantz and Guildenstern to accompany Hamlet to England. Alone, Claudius tries to repent but cannot. Hamlet, summoned to Gertrude's room as Polonius planned, sees the King apparently at prayer, but refuses to kill him lest he should send his soul to heaven.

Commentary

Instructing Rosencrantz and Guildenstern, the King consolidates his counter-plot. Polonius's entry keeps you keyed up for the meeting of Hamlet with his mother (27-9), while Shakespeare pursues the effect of the play scene on Claudius.

The King's soliloquy shows him as a *man* of dual nature: a murderer, but with an active conscience. The self-searching process of his honest wrestling towards prayer encourages you to reassess Hamlet's stock 'villain'. The irresolution keeping Claudius from prayer (39-43) while Hamlet responds to 'blasts from hell', depicts antagonists having more in common than you would have supposed.

Through a series of interlocking questions and answers the soliloquy debates the central issue of the scope of prayer and divine mercy for a criminal acknowledging his guilt, but incapable of active contrition. Its hammering monosyllabic style, with its reversed or bunched stresses ('Pray can I not'), quite unlike the smooth flow of Claudius's public persona, is apt to his inner conflict.

Hamlet's unexpected entry makes the dramatic temperature soar. The stage picture of Hamlet with sword drawn raises the obvious question, will he take his revenge? Its recall of Pyrrhus's savage slaughter of Priam at the altar, and Hamlet's fifth soliloquy, prompt the further question, should he? The opportunity is sheathed with Hamlet's sword, and the questions are answered by his sixth soliloquy.

This soliloquy is a natural sequel to his embracing of evil in his fifth. Hamlet, refusing to kill the King until he can do so in a way that damns his soul, has given great offence to those who want Hamlet to be a purely noble tragic hero. But psychoanalysing it as bravado covering revulsion from killing a defenceless man at prayer, or an excuse for further delay (see Arden edn, LN to III.iii.89–95, pp.513–14) has no support from the text. Each speaker is aware of the irony of his dilemma: the King, of the ruin of his spiritual hopes if he retains 'those effects' for which he 'did the murder', and of his earthly power if he does not; Hamlet, of self-defeat and defeat of justice for his father, cuts off without absolution, if he sends his killer to heaven and his own soul to hell. Irony resides in each character speaking in ignorance: Claudius of Hamlet's presence; each, of what is in the other's mind. But Shakespeare tops this with a further level of irony. Not until Hamlet's exit does he reveal the climactic irony in Claudius's clinching couplet

> My words fly up, my thoughts remain below.
> Words without thoughts never to heaven go

that Claudius's attempt to pray has failed while Hamlet has refrained from killing him for fear he should not be damned. Along with Hamlet, we have been deceived by appearance. To have the perfect opportunity for revenge thwarted by the revenge code stresses both the repulsiveness and inadequacy of that code to the moral dilemmas assailing Hamlet's double-sided nature in his double-sided task.

Act III, Scene iv

Summary
In the Queen's closet, Gertrude, alarmed by Hamlet's violence, calls for help. Polonius, echoing her cry behind the arras, is killed by Hamlet. The Ghost appears, unseen by Gertrude, to remind Hamlet of his prior task to pursue revenge on Claudius. Hamlet succeeds in stirring Gertrude's con-

science, appeals to her to forsake his uncle's bed, and admits he is but 'mad in craft'.

Commentary
Scene iv presents, in four sections, the good-and-evil consequences of Hamlet's 'hellish' impulses. His killing of Polonius is the pivot that sets the action towards tragic catastrophe and his full acceptance of his dual role. This 'rash and bloody deed' which he did not intend (for Polonius) is balanced by the stirring of his mother's conscience, which he did. Contrast the Queen's willingness to repent with the King's determination to hang on to his 'effects'. The Ghost's second visit points what Hamlet has *not* done, the Queen's lack of perception, and 'assurance of a man' in a scene where the beast in man has threatened to overwhelm the god.

Hamlet's planned attack on his mother's conscience is no sooner begun than interrupted by the unexpected violence of Polonius's killing. Hamlet's rough violence, 'Come . . . sit you down, you shall not budge', the Queen's alarm echoed by Polonius, and the visiting of Hamlet's displaced frenzy on the eavesdropping 'rat', combine in one lightning stage-image of the instinctive behaviour of animals in a crisis.

The Queen's 'What hast thou done?' asks from us an answer beyond Hamlet's uncertain 'I know not. Is it the King?' His deed is a structural hinge that changes everything. The killing of Claudius's chief minister puts Hamlet in his power, and makes Hamlet's death imperative for him. The catastrophe to Polonius's meddling starts a second revenge action in which 'the hero charged with . . . vengeance now also incurs vengeance' (Arden edn,p.144) and achieves tragic recognition of his dual nature and dual role, glimpsed here as he contemplates Polonius's body (175-7). He accepts that 'Heaven' punishing 'me with this and this with me' has destined him to be its 'scourge and minister'.

When the confrontation with his mother resumes, the words 'to kill a King and marry with his brother' (27-8) are not so much Hamlet's test of her complicity in King Hamlet's murder as a merging of Claudius's murder with Gertrude's of the god in man when she abandoned 'Hyperion' for the 'satyr'.

The next section (53-67) employs two stage props (probably miniature portraits) to develop the god/beast antithesis between the brother kings. How does this device answer Gertrude's 'What have I done?' The re-creation of the complete man prepares us for his apparition; awakens from 'bestial oblivion' Gertrude's conscience, and counterbalances Hamlet's imagery of bestial sex and his killing a man in sudden passion while attempting – successfully – to save his mother's soul.

The Ghost, a dramatic shock, swings attention back to the revenge plot. Its 'gracious figure' reminds Hamlet of his duty to his father (110-11) and his courtesy to his mother (112-15), obscured by his vehement obsession with sexuality. In this strange family reunion, the Ghost measures different levels of perception. Ghosts could choose who should and should not see them, and Gertrude's blindness is necessary to the plot. Directors who banish the Ghost from the stage destroy the contrast, and leave the audience, like the Queen, supposing it a figment of Hamlet's distracted imagination. Gertrude must not flatter herself that his madness, not her trespass, speaks (148-9). The Ghost's visitation at once changes Hamlet's tone. It is marked by control of his sexual obsession, awareness of his mother's limitations, and of his own in directing souls, and trust, when he divulges the secret of his feigned madness.

The scene closes strongly, with a suggestion of order coming out of disorder. After the reversal of natural order (son chiding mother) Hamlet's 'when you are desirous to be blest/I'll blessing beg of you' promises his return to order. His repentant shouldering of responsibility for Polonius's death (174-9) brings a cosmic sense of order in his first recognition of himself as an agent under Heaven's direction. The final dialogue (202-19) consolidates Hamlet's trust in his mother when he confides his plans and his knowledge of the King's. In the revenge plot we are left awaiting the outcome of his imprecise and Claudius's precise plans in the kind of design hinted at 'when in one line two crafts directly meet'.

Act IV divides into two main parts: Scenes i, ii, iii leading to Hamlet's departure for England, with Scene iv as a bridge to v, vi, vii detailing events at Elsinore in his absence. Some very short scenes will not be considered under separate headings.

Act IV, Scenes i, ii, iii

Summary
To the King, Gertrude blames Polonius's death on Hamlet's madness. Claudius orders Rosencrantz and Guildenstern to apprehend him, and gives Hamlet his sailing orders. He reveals in a soliloquy that sealed orders instruct the English King to execute Hamlet.

Commentary
A succession of short scenes, dominated by Claudius, dramatises the speed with which the action to hunt down Hamlet moves under his direction. Yet Shakespeare's structure discloses a double movement that questions Claudius's control. On the one hand the recurrent hunt metaphor is realised in Hamlet at bay. He is brought, a prisoner, to trial before the King, whose soliloquy (iii.61-71) reveals that his sentence of exile conceals sentence of death. Yet as Claudius's power increases so does Hamlet's power to undercut the dignity of his captors. With the Queen on stage between Hamlet's exit and Claudius's entry, the action is continuous. Yet in IV.i the beginning of a new movement can be felt. Signs of grace appear in the Queen. How does she 'translate' to the King Hamlet's killing of Polonius while preserving loyalty to her son? The King's repeated, and

ignored, 'Come away' could hint at estrangement. Gertrude's new strength, moreover, is countered by further signs of weakness in Claudius: 'My soul is full of discord and dismay'. Their contrasted response to Polonius's death warms us to the Queen and distances us from the King. Gertrude's generous 'good old man' contrasts with the King's repeated concern for his own safety – 'It had been so with us had we been there' – and reputation – 'It will be laid to us'. He ends the scene once again the practical politician, persuading Gertrude he is acting out of care for the state, herself, and Hamlet.

Between two scenes demonstrating the King's actions to bring the 'criminal' Hamlet to justice, IV.ii undercuts the value of both action and authority with black comedy. First, the hunt for Polonius's body, which links all three scenes, focuses the question whether death makes action meaningless, man 'a thing . . . of nothing'. Reverent and irreverent ways of coping with death are indicated in 'bring the body/Into the Chapel' (IV.i.36-7) and 'Safely stowed' (IV.ii.1). Secondly, Hamlet continues the deflation of the King's authority by dehumanising imagery, of the King as an ape chewing the 'sponges' of his tame officers, which he will squeeze dry of his delegated authority when he no longer needs them, and finally as a 'thing . . of nothing', either as man or King. The reduction to absurdity of Hamlet's adversaries contrasts with his own growing stature. The metaphorical distance he puts between the 'sponge' and the 'son of a king' (11-12) links him with the noble king we have just seen again in III.iv.

Approaching IV.iii, our view of the antagonists in action, separately, in IV.i and IV.ii makes us wonder what kind of conflict they will engage in when face to face. At first (1-45) the two adversaries behave predictably: Claudius keeping up a reasonable front, Hamlet throwing out barbed jests under cover of his antic disposition. The people's love of Hamlet, which has tied his adversary's hands, is a new motif introduced here to enhance his developing stature. Yet Claudius, wiser than Rosencrantz and Guildenstern in his ignoring of personal insults, resists the threat of Hamlet's antic comments to disrupt the orderly proceedings, and, refusing to be deflected, finally gets the answer to 'Where is Polonius?' his minions were denied. But, diminishing him to the audience, Hamlet dwells increasingly on the physical corruption of death that levels kings and beggars (19-31).

The duel takes on a new edge when we learn from two ding-dong exchanges, constituting an iambic pentameter, that all is set:

KING For England./HAM. For England?/KING Ay, Hamlet./HAM. Good.

It launches an electrically-charged dialogue (46-56) where dramatic irony depends on your knowing that each speaker understands his opponent's warning sub-text beneath the neutral words. The crisp exchange and succeeding dialogue:

KING So is it, if thou knew'st our purposes.
HAMLET I see a cherub that sees them. But come, for England.

contribute to the ever-more-insistent theme of contrary purposes working towards Heaven's design. Hamlet's eagerness for the voyage away from his 'prison' augurs a change in the situation. The more that there is to see, which Hamlet is satisfied Heaven will see though he himself may not, is revealed in the soliloquy concluding this stage of the conflict (61-71), where Claudius, dropping the mask of grieved father and just King, reveals his true purpose – Hamlet's death.

Act IV, Scene iv

Summary
On the way to embark for England, Hamlet observes Fortinbras and his army passing peacefully through Denmark to win back a paltry patch of ground from Poland. Fortinbras's action triggers off another soliloquy of self-reproach for his own inaction.

Commentary
The Fortinbras scene and the soliloquy it elicits from Hamlet are often cut in performance. Yet IV.iv is a needful bridge between past and future. The audience must be reminded of Fortinbras, last referred to in II.ii, and not to appear again until V.ii to take the Danish throne. With Fortinbras on stage, emphasis moves from the inactive to the active hero, one of Hamlet's mirror images. Hamlet's entry on Fortinbras's exit revives comparison between them: one who has forgone his revenge for a father; the other who has yet to achieve it. Both have grown in stature: Fortinbras from the headstrong youth leading 'lawless resolutes' to the royal general heading his army in disciplined march over the stage. A near-meeting between them prompts continued comparison between the tragic hero with his complex nature and destiny of victor and victim, and the destined conqueror, heroical by the world's simplified values, and no questions asked about casualties. The re-entry of one of Hamlet's simplified mirror-images anticipates the re-entry of the other, Laertes, in the next scene, and renewed comparisons of all three. Hamlet's astonishment, on questioning the captain (9-29), that two armies will 'debate the question of this straw' suggests a questioning of Fortinbras's simple code of honour, even while the soliloquy shows he envies it. The audience needs a final soliloquy from Hamlet at this point to make a powerful impression that will survive his absence from the next three scenes. Outmanoeuvred by Claudius on the practical front, and while the consequences of his evil phase (Ophelia's madness and death, Laertes seeking revenge) are displayed, he needs to retain our sympathies by a persisting image of his resolution, idealism and moral awareness. A soldier's double role is an apt 'occasion' to recall the moral questions Hamlet has grappled with since Act I, on how to kill without tainting his mind.

To observe the advances which prepare for a changed Hamlet to return from his voyage, compare his soliloquy closely with 'O what a rogue and peasant slave am I' (II.ii.543–601). Both are soliloquies of self-reproach; both show Hamlet trying to understand his delay in executing revenge. Both are prompted by the powerful effect of an illusion; one, the Player's identification with a 'dream of passion', the other, the 'fantasy and trick of fame' which inspires men to fight for 'an eggshell'. Actor and soldier share a commitment to their role which in Hamlet's eyes brands him a 'dull and muddy-mettled rascal'. The first prompts Hamlet to charge himself with inadequacies of feeling, the second, of inadequacies of the 'reason' which should spur him to action. And though Hamlet's position in the two soliloquies looks similar, the second, in the process of tightly-structured thinking, shows him developing a new maturity. The 'occasion' that informs against him, Fortinbras's firing his men, in pursuit of a 'fantasy', to rise superior to the fear of death, leads him to see that right action must be spurred by 'excitements of . . . reason' as well as the 'blood' he envied in the Player. To admit, having weighed alternative explanations (40-1), that he *does not know*, although he has 'cause, and will, and strength, and means to do it', why 'this thing' is still 'to do', implies an error in his measurement of himself against absolute standards which brand him coward, and prepares for his unquestioning trust in Providence's purposes. From this climax the inappropriateness of the 'examples' that exhort him is suggested by ambiguous language that carries criticism as well as admiration for Fortinbras's enterprise of honour, and wonder at man's mind which invests a valueless object with value worth dying for. The conclusion that 'rightly to be great' is 'greatly to find quarrel in a straw/When honour's at the stake' admits both the creative and destructive face of Fortinbras's heroic code. A strong image points the disproportion in the 'twenty thousand men' whose slain bodies the 'plot of land' is not 'tomb enough . . . to hide'. In his exit, it is his *thoughts* that Hamlet dedicates to his revenger's task, demonstrating the essential lesson he has sifted out of Fortinbras's honour, which he is to adapt to the Player-King's wisdom, *'Our thoughts are ours, their ends none of our own'*.

This final soliloquy affords opportunity to consider the purpose of the whole sequence of Hamlet's soliloquies. The large number – seven – reflects the importance of Hamlet's inner world as a touchstone of integrity set against the deception of Claudius's corrupt public world. The convention of soliloquy establishes a confidential relationship between character and audience; he tells you the truth, but only such partial and subjective truth as he knows about himself. Consider how Hamlet's responses to various 'occasions' record his journey, at seven stages of his dramatic situation, towards a meaning in life and his role in it. Follow him from his initial recoil from 'sullied flesh', the endeavour to keep good and evil separate, through the precise balance of pros and cons for living in 'To be or not to be' followed by temporary submission to 'blasts from hell' in the fifth and

sixth soliloquies, to a final recognition of both the ambiguity and necessity
of action, well thought out, in a cause he is to see later as greater than
personal revenge or honour.

Act IV, Scene v

Summary
Ophelia, driven mad with grief, sings ballad snatches before the King and
Queen which re-enact her double loss of Hamlet and Polonius. Upon her
exit Laertes enters at the head of a rebellious mob, seeking revenge for his
father's death. Ophelia's second appearance strengthens his resolution. The
King promises to reveal the true culprit.

Commentary
The action from IV.v onward is master-minded by Claudius, with the
significant exception of IV.vi, Hamlet's letter to Horatio. IV.v presents
Claudius with a double crisis and keeps the absent Hamlet in mind by
showing the realted consequences of his killing of Polonius: Ophelia's
madness, and Laertes' return from France to revenge them both in the
second revenge action that leads to the tragic catastrophe.

Ophelia's lyrical madness gives relief in tone from the intense build-up
of play scene, closet scene, and hunt, demonstrates the Queen's continuing
sense of guilt, and exposes the King's inadequacy in dealing with mental
breakdown contrasted with his cool proficiency in quelling incipient social
breakdown. Action and imagery point to central themes: uncertainties of
identity and reputation, remembrance, appearance and reality, role-playing,
the closeness of love and death, the recoil pattern, order and disorder;
above all, the inexorable growth of evil which resists all attempts to hide
it. We are invited to compare the two revengers (with Fortinbras and
Pyrrhus implied), the two women, together for the first time since the
play scene, and Ophelia's real with Hamlet's simulated madness.

The theme of remembrance unites the Ophelia and Laertes episodes.
The memory of the past has driven Ophelia mad, Laertes to revenge, and
the Queen to remorse. It brings cause and consequence together in vivid
stage images which contrast poignantly with the happy family scene of
I.iii. Ophelia's distracted appearance before the King and Queen (21–73)
demonstrates one consequence of their sins.

As guides to the 'method' in Ophelia's madness, Shakespeare places
signposts. In Hamlet's pretence of madness, Hamlet is conscious of much
of the 'method', though some is Shakespeare's and not his. In Ophelia's, it
is all Shakespeare's. Ophelia's unconsciousness of her company and sur-
roundings distinguishes from the satirical ambivalence of Hamlet's 'antic
disposition' the pathos of her real madness. Cues that invite you to look
for sub-textual meaning in her 'unshaped' speech include the anonymous

gentleman's prelude (4–13), the Queen's 'what imports this song?' and Ophelia's reiterated 'pray you mark'. On her second appearance, Laertes' comments, 'a document in madness', 'this nothing's more than matter', invite you to reflect what 'more' it 'documents', and develops for him a choric function. The King's naming the cause as 'Conceit upon her father' is a half-truth exposed by Ophelia's preoccupation also with her lover.

The Queen's aside in the prelude to Ophelia's first entry stresses the 'guilt' that makes her 'sick soul' unwilling to witness the consequences of her sexual frailty. Hamlet's merging of guilty and innocent women here receives its crowning irony when Ophelia unconsciously plays out her fantasies of sexual fulfilment in front of the Queen whose sexual appetite condemned her to virginity. Freed from rational control, Ophelia's deepest self confusedly enacts through traditional ballad and snatches of ritual the funeral denied to her father and the fulfilment in love denied to her. Her attempts go some way towards restoring the dignity which is threatened by a grotesque perspective (IV.i, ii, iii) that places man with beast. Her unfulfilment and fantasy of fulfilment motivate her two songs and the mental figment of the coach and attendant ladies she would have had as Hamlet's wife (71–3). That imagined royalty is more real to her than the appearance of it in the King and Queen, whose nothingness reveals itself in their futile attempts to stop her flow. The first ballad, *'How should I your true love know'* links the innocent singer with the Queen, whose failure to distinguish her true love *'from another one'* has driven Hamlet melancholy and Ophelia mad. The King's entry is appropriately marked by the robust song of a seducer and his willing lady, *'Tomorrow is St. Valentine's day'* (48–66), ironically reflecting the needless warning of Ophelia's father and brother (I.iii) against Hamlet's courtship.

Shakespeare modifies the sadness of the scene by an exit speech for Ophelia combining a renewed stab of grief for her father with a hint – in 'I hope all will be well. We must be patient' – of some design in life which contains, without compensating for, her suffering; and, in yet another key, of Laertes' return to avenge his family's wrongs (70). With Horatio's exit to keep watch on her the King's speech to Gertrude (75–96) conveys new information necessary to the Laertes plot. It is conveyed dramatically, through the King's character reacting to his present situation. We respond to Claudius's genuine concern for 'Poor Ophelia'; to his vulnerable need for Gertrude, expressed in urgent repetition of her name (77,96); to his unusual depression stemming from disorders in the state; and to the honesty that admits to error in Polonius's 'hugger-mugger' burial. Yet our critical judgment notes his distortions and concealments: her father's death as sufficient explanation of Ophelia's madness; Hamlet's homicide justifying his 'remove'; and the imagery of 'mere beasts', 'poison', and the rapid spread of 'pestilent' accounts which ironically tell another story – of hidden evil surfacing through 'hugger-mugger' proceedings to infect the innocent and recoil on the guilty.

Shakespeare builds up to Laertes' stormy entry with dramatic economy: the messenger's image of the ocean overflowing its banks, '*noise within*' and Laertes at the door bidding a few visible rebels 'stand . . . all without'. Like Fortinbras in Act I, Laertes is a political threat to a state already infected with disorder. The confrontation of Laertes and Claudius (112–52) restores Claudius's identity as a diplomatic monarch and the silent Gertrude as a woman courageous where she loves. The King's reiterated 'Let him go, Gertrude' frames his confident statement of the divine protection of kings (122–6). We can admire the calm courage and the reasoned argument with which Claudius deflates Laertes' 'giant-like' bombast, while savouring the irony that it is Claudius, killer of a king and shortly to be killed himself, who quotes the divine protection of kings.

The major purpose of this Laertes episode, and the characterisation of him here and in the next scene, is to present him as a foil to Hamlet; the perfect revenger of conventional revenge drama. Hamlet tested Claudius's guilt: Laertes charges him recklessly with guilt of which he is innocent. Laertes consigns 'to the profoundest pit' such conscience as, with respect to the after-life, gave Hamlet 'pause'. His ranting, close to caricature, warns you against uncritical admiration for the drive which shortly has him serving the King's will, not Heaven's. Negligent of 'both the worlds', risking civil war, ready to 'dare damnation', cut Hamlet's throat 'i'th' church', and soon to welcome and improve upon dishonourable means to revenge, this revenger makes you think more favourably of Hamlet's scrupulous caution.

Repetition of '*noise within*' and 'Let her come in' herald Ophelia's second appearance. Consider Laertes' response. It indicates a young man with more facets to his character than his stock revenger pose would suggest. His swings of feeling from hyperbole (154–5), through determination to avenge this new sorrow (156–7), anguished love finding expression in broken phrases, to sententious reflection (159–63) foreshadow the young man who is not as ruthless as he backs himself to be; who weeps at the Queen's account of Ophelia's death (IV.v.185–90) and admits 'it is almost against [his] conscience' to give Hamlet his death-blow (V.ii.300). Laertes' second role, as choric commentator to the spectacle of Ophelia's distribution of flowers, guides us to a correct interpretation.

As first recipient of Ophelia's flowers, Laertes gives us a lead in accepting the emblematic meaning she offers: 'thoughts and remembrance fitted'. Assuming the emblematic significance of flowers for an Elizabethan audience, critics and directors have found problems in who receives which flowers. Ophelia's occasional assignment of another role – lover, brother, father – to the unrecognised people before her adds to the confusion. If fennel (flattery) and columbine (marital infidelity) are given to the Queen, recalling the Ghost's account of her winning by Claudius's seductive wit (I.v.45–7), and rue to the King who has shown his need for repentance, as the innocent Ophelia embraces its sorrow, their sexual transgressions are rebuked by a voice, like the Ghost's, which is already beyond this world.

The rosemary she gives to her brother, merged in her faulty remembrance with her lover – 'pray, love, remember' – with its dual association of remembrance between lovers and of the dead, makes the gentle Ophelia unwittingly play the same role in her brother's revenge as the Ghost ('Remember me') plays in Hamlet's – a loaded irony. Directors who furnish Ophelia only with imaginary flowers make nonsense of Laertes' 'thoughts and remembrance fitted', and detract from the visual spectacle. The beauty of real flowers reinforces the positive value of Ophelia, pointed by Laertes, to turn affliction, 'hell itself . . . to favour and to prettiness', contrasting the jaundiced vision of Hamlet.

Ophelia's departure from the stage to a musical motif of mingled joy ('*Bonny sweet Robin*') in love and the finality of its loss ('*He never will come again*') prepares for the paradox of her happy death. It closes the lyrical interlude to give place to the King's offer to give Laertes 'due content' – meaning, to us, not only his account of Polonius's death, but the scheme for Hamlet's assassination.

Act IV, Scenes vi, vii

Summary

In Scene vi sailors bring a letter for Horatio from Hamlet, announcing his return, aided by pirates who had captured him. In Scene vii Claudius, learning of the failure of his first scheme to kill Hamlet, plots a second with Laertes by which Laertes can achieve his revenge. They arrange that he should kill Hamlet, as by accident, in a fencing match with an unblunted poison-tipped foil, backed up with a poisoned drink. The Queen reports Ophelia's death by drowning.

Commentary

Hamlet's letter to Horatio, a welcome interlude in plain prose between the lyric madness of Ophelia and the King's sinister plotting with Laertes, gives a preview of the counter-threat to their unholy alliance. It allays fears of Hamlet's plotted death in England, and prepares for his return. His presence of mind in concealing his identity, striking a bargain with the pirates, and exploiting a chance 'occasion' not for self-reproach but, with Claudius's murderous scheme frustrated, to take him back to his duty of revenge in Denmark, augurs well for its accomplishment.

Scene vii prepares for the catastrophe in two ways: plot-wise, through the King's evil persuasion of Laertes into the second scheme against Hamlet's life, and in mood, through the sad waste of Ophelia's death. We are gripped by the King's masterly tactics and Laertes' corruption, under their spell, from an honest if ruthless avenger to an eager accomplice in treacherous cold-blooded murder.

The scene falls into three sections, divided by two messengers who significantly interrupt human planning with news of events unplanned, but made inevitable by a chain of sin: the first, Hamlet's return; the second, Ophelia's death. Lines 1-35 prepare the ground for the alliance of the King and Laertes. At this stage Laertes holds your sympathy by his lament (25-9) for the perfect sister lost to him, and his straightforward acceptance of the King's deceptive reasoning on why he has not brought Hamlet to public justice. The messenger with letters comes on cue, the King supposes, to fulfil his promise to Laertes, 'You shortly shall hear more' - namely that his revenge has been anticipated. Our foreknowledge of Hamlet's return enables us to savour the irony of the two men's different reactions to the news: in Laertes, renewed hope of personal vengeance; in the King, initially, confusion between appearance and reality ('is it some abuse, and no such thing?') followed by the groping towards a new plot, now urgently necessary, using the younger man's purpose to achieve his own. Hesitancies, indirections, and directions disguise his evil intent under a veneer of reason.

The King's description of Lamord's horsemanship, apparently a digression, fulfils several functions. It is one of the small touches which restore Hamlet to the world of Renaissance courtly accomplishment of which he was, said Ophelia, 'the expectancy and rose'; and in which, with his alleged competitive interest in Laertes' repute as a fencer, it is natural for him to accept the wager upon their skills. The perfect fusion of man and beast in Lamord's control of his horse images once again that co-existence of the human and the bestial which is central to the play. Common knowledge of the Norman encourages an alliance between the King and the young man he is flattering with this expert courtier's praise. Above all, the name of this 'wondrous' messenger in its similarity to 'La Mort' chills the blood with a premonition of death for the three men to whom he is thematically connected.

With the King's 'Now out of this—' (104) we expect the plot will at last get moving again. But his temptation of Laertes proceeds by yet another flank attack and apparent digression. Switching from flattery to assail the vulnerability Laertes has just shown to family love, he demands, directly, 'Laertes, was your father dear to you?' Laertes rises to the bait, with an extreme claim of what he 'would . . . undertake' to show himself his father's son.

The direct pounce of 'Hamlet comes back' which at last comes to the 'quick of th'ulcer' and elicits Laertes' savage readiness 'To cut his throat i'th'church' (125), introduces the King's plan for the fencing match in which Laertes is to give Hamlet his death-wound with an unbated weapon. The needs of the plot are paramount here. The detailed scenario frees our minds at the fencing match itself to note whether their 'drift' will 'look through' their 'performance', and to note Providence's redirection of their 'props' - poisoned cup and sword - to ends that improve on their evil purposes. A secondary function is to prove how thoroughly Laertes is now the King's man. His preference for open confrontation (55-6) – not suiting the King's need to protect his secret – gives way easily to the King's for a 'pass of practice', and improves on it with his idea to tip the sword with poison.

The contempt for sacred things shown in their language indicates a rejection of Heaven's prompting now offset by the Queen's report of Ophelia's death (162-82). Ophelia's connection with Heaven and its forgiveness, expressed here in the 'lauds' she sings while drowning, points the contrast with her brother's prostitution of his sacred duty of revenge to the hellish scheme of Claudius. The Queen assumes a role usually given to a messenger of humbler rank to clinch the thematic connection between her and Ophelia. The pity and beauty of her speech restore her to a human dignity which Hamlet's revolting animal images took from her in the closet scene. Her report vividly re-creates an offstage event. The realistic detail 'an envious sliver broke' gives the lie to the verdict of suicide preferred in V.i by gravedigger and 'churlish priest'. The weeping willow, emblem of forsaken love, and appropriate weeds and flowers, repeat, in keeping with her ballad snatches, Ophelia's associations with innocence, love, death: an epitome of the life process. As a sequel to her mad songs, the report of her death complements in a lyric key the hints of approaching catastrophe by the preceding 'deep plots'.

Act V, Scene i

Summary
Hamlet, philosophising on mortality with a gravedigger, learns through observing Laertes' grief that the grave is Ophelia's. Hamlet reveals himself at the funeral, the two young men fight on Ophelia's coffin and are parted.

Commentary
The graveyard scene explores in both comic and serious modes the significance of death and consequently of life. It demonstrates Hamlet's more balanced attitude to the life process by confronting him with a series of challenges, concluding with the aggression of Laertes. The scene falls into three sections: the comic prelude to Hamlet's arrival, his dialogue with Horatio and then with the gravedigger on the unearthed skulls, Ophelia's funeral and its sequel. In 1–60 Shakespeare's comic treatment of serious themes through the two Clowns counterpoints without displacing the build-up to the play's tragic climax. Their workaday approach to dead bodies presents one of death's many faces. Their dialogue combines expectation (the grave will be Ophelia's) with surprise (after the eyewitness report of accidental death, the suspicion of suicide). The Gravedigger's song introducing and later punctuating Hamlet's dialogue with Horatio (61–115), in its theme of the inevitable decay of life and love a sequel to Ophelia's songs in IV.v, connects the two centres of attention on stage as its sound draws Ophelia's cruel lover towards her grave.

Hamlet's tone of amused, but not unbalanced, disgust – 'Has this fellow no feeling of his business a sings in grave-making?' – prompts questions about the change in him hinted at in his letter to Horatio. The change and 'readiness' for his task are tested here (74–210) in a way not encompassed by bustling activity on the high seas. In its first form, death as every man's fate, the test is posed by the Gravedigger's stage business of clearing the grave of its past occupants during Hamlet's dialogue with Horatio. It provides both stimulus for Hamlet's flights of fancy on the skulls thrown up at intervals, and an ironic comment on his soaring imagination in physical evidence of the mortality that completes the human paradox.

Shakespeare postpones the climax to this series of skulls – Yorick's – by an apparent digression concerning the Gravedigger's length of service (138–57). Its importance lies not in fixing Hamlet's age at thirty (157) for literalist critics (see 6.1, 'Problems and non-problems') but in the double perspective it gives of man's life in its greatness and littleness. 'Thirty years' evokes a lifetime's span, 'man and boy', rather than an accurate number of years. It telescopes the opposite ends of life to question its purpose with the economy of Samuel Beckett: 'They give birth astride of a grave, the light gleams an instant, then it's night once more' (*Waiting for Godot*).

Two forms of the confrontation with mortality remain to evaluate Hamlet's purpose and his 'readiness' to achieve it; dramatised in a skull he knew and a body he loved. His question 'How long will a man lie i' the' earth ere he rot?', answered by the Gravedigger's professional interest in the keeping properties of corpses, narrows Hamlet's contemplation to the physical corruption and inevitable end that every man is born to; which throughout the play has been an image of its cause and counterpart, original sin. His share in corruption, mortality, and their threat of meaninglessness, Hamlet must accept as victim of man's common destiny before he can cleanse the kingdom of Claudius, a more active sinner than himself.

The jester's skull is a well-chosen dramatic surprise. In this one stage prop, which Hamlet holds in his hand (no longer a distant onlooker), Shakespeare encapsulates the dual nature and destiny no man can escape. In life Yorick was 'a fellow of *infinite* jest' and now, the 'quintessence of dust'. Hamlet's response is also two-sided. Both terms of the opposition are necessary to define the worth of being human; a lesson Hamlet has learnt when he affirms his love for Ophelia at her grave.

On the ironically imagined fate of dead Alexander and Caesar (191–209) Hamlet's tone of mingled humour and serenity indicates a determination to cope through laughter with the paradox that has inspired so much serious meditation. The ebullient logic of Hamlet's propositions about the re-cycling of Alexander and Caesar having diverted us from the arrival we expected, Ophelia's funeral bell shatters the lightened mood.

This, the second test of Hamlet's readiness for the execution of his task, puts a severe strain on the balanced perspective he has just achieved. Yorick has been dead for a generation; his love and rejection of Ophelia are fresh in mind. The ritual centred on her grave again has Hamlet commenting from the sidelines. Ritual, however, 'maimed', affirms human worth. Ophelia's survives the churlishness of the priest who would have buried her, a possible suicide, 'in ground unsanctified', and the shocking fight of her brother and lover on top of her coffin. Hamlet's short functional commentary (210-15) contrasts with his expansive meditations on the skulls. His step-by-step groping towards what we already know builds suspense for his final realisation of who lies in the coffin.

Ophelia's funeral, as it takes centre stage, throws out numerous connections, like the Gravedigger's work, to Hamlet on the sidelines. Her 'virgin crants' and 'maiden strewments' are visible emblems of their linked tragedies, Hamlet's revulsion from breeding causing her unfulfilment in love and marriage. Laertes' wish that violets may spring from 'flesh' only 'unpolluted' because she died before breeding sinners, connects the end of their love story with its beginning in Laertes' warning (I.iii) against Hamlet's young love as a violet, and its withering into madness and death, when the violets she would give had withered after her father died. The Queen's strewing of flowers on the coffin completes the correspondences shown between Hamlet's mother and Hamlet's true-love. Her utterance of unfulfilled hopes, that Ophelia should 'have been my Hamlet's wife' (237) impinges on the concealed Hamlet, thus made aware of what he has missed through Polonius's worldly interpretation of his courtship; and on Laertes, re-fuelling his hatred of the man he holds responsible for his sister's death.

Ophelia's funeral brings Hamlet's future killer into prominence, affording further comparisons between the two revengers who are destined to kill each other. At first Laertes' rebuke to the 'churlish priest' and the simple moving language of his farewell to his sister (231-5) invite sympathy. All the more startling is his outburst of 'rant' (239-47) and melodramatic leap into the grave. Hamlet's majestic scorn of Laertes' superman acting of the stock 'hero' role, too simple to represent the truth of life's many-sidedness and littleness which the graveyard had rammed home, prompts two vital recognitions to which the whole play moves. 'This is I,/Hamlet the Dane' (its climactic certainty opposing '*What* is he . . .?' – the role-player), and 'I lov'd Ophelia' (264) demonstrate Hamlet's complete acceptance of life's intertwined good and evil. His claim to the royal title ('the Dane') not only indicates a scarcely-veiled threat to the King but acknowledges a share (though not an equal share) in Claudius's sinful nature, and his rightful place as 'native' (I.iv.14) and heir to man's kingdom of sullied flesh. In dealing with Laertes' murderous assault, though he is to regret that, provoked to 'tow'ring passion', he 'forgot himself' (V.ii.75-80), Hamlet's restraint ('*prithee* take thy fingers from my throat') compares favourably with Laertes' murderous hysteria.

Why does Shakespeare conclude the scene with a reminder that everyone is 'acting'? The King's and Queen's assurances to Laertes that Hamlet is mad are obviously false for different reasons. Hamlet, quickly abandoning a sincere appeal ('I lov'd you ever') to Laertes, whose black and white view of 'love' can hardly comprehend the kind that kills his father and drives his sister mad, takes refuge in the 'antic disposition' expected of him (286-7). The King's concluding speech (289-94) is a piece of quick-change role-playing that relies on discrepancies of awareness between characters and audience. The concerned step-father appears in his requests to Horatio and Gertrude (heard by everyone) to keep watch on Hamlet. Aside to Laertes, a reminder of 'our last night's speech' makes sense only to Laertes and the Globe audience. 'This grave shall have a living monument' carries a public meaning to the court and a private, sinister implication to Laertes and the audience.

The uses of prose and verse in this scene are instructive. Hamlet's speaking of both is influenced by his context. An easy though distinctive prose style links him to the macabre comedy of the Gravedigger: a change to blank verse suits Ophelia's funeral. The verse, like the prose, embraces a wide range: from Hamlet's 'mad' couplet and Laertes' hysterical rant, and Hamlet's burlesque of it, to the priest's liturgical cadences, Hamlet's majestic claim to the kingdom, and measured restraint in repelling Laertes' aggression. Hamlet's use of blank verse in this scene marks his return to the form for public utterance for the first time since I.ii. Apart from the 'mad' couplet meant to mislead, he speaks nothing in verse which is not an honest expression of his true self. His resumption of verse indicates the integration of the Prince with his public role as cleanser of the kingdom.

Act V, Scene ii

Summary
Hamlet tells Horatio how he arranged for the execution of Rosencrantz and Guildenstern instead of his own. He accepts the King's invitation to a fencing match with Laertes, brought by an affected courtier, Osric. In the match the foils are exchanged in a scuffle, causing a fatal wound to each combatant. Gertrude drinks the poisoned wine intended for Hamlet and dies. Laertes dies confessing the plot. Hamlet stabs Claudius and forces poisoned wine down his throat, giving Fortinbras his dying voice for election as King. Fortinbras enters with the English ambassadors, who report that Rosencrantz and Guildenstern are dead. Fortinbras orders a heroic funeral for Hamlet.

Commentary
V.i and ii keep ineradicable and eradicable corruption in fruitful tension. The common doom's apparent denial of meaning in the graveyard scene is now challenged by Hamlet's initiative, employing the 'interim' life allows, to halt the spread of evil, killing Claudius, 'this canker of our nature'. He expiates in death the guilt inseparable from his own nature and fulfils both that and his predominant nobility. The audience is shown the larger design of Providence using antithetical human purposes and apparent accidents (the exchange of rapiers, Gertrude drinking the poisoned wine) to achieve its aim in cleansing the kingdom.

In Hamlet's promised report to Horatio (3-55) his unrepented ruthlessness towards his old schoolfellows anticipates the fulfilment of his revenge without further reluctance. We follow his experience of perceiving 'a divinity' shaping the events of his voyage into a meaningful design beyond personal 'ends', 'rough-hew them how we will', transforming him into an active and willing partner of Providence. Hamlet's hunch to investigate the commission, followed by a lightning plan of action without 'prologue', suggests attention to Providential promptings. In his having by chance his royal father's ring to seal the forged commission he sees 'heaven ordinant'. But chance and intuitive hunches need an active contribution from Hamlet. His strategem, though 'begun' by Providential prompting, requires a cool head, resourcefulness, courage, and ruthlessness. 'The next day/... our sea-fight', a providential chance, depends for its outcome on Hamlet's initiative.

Just before Hamlet's heroic side takes the ascendant in the fencing match, you are shown 'Hamlet the Dane' as a player-king using the world's deceptive skills to play its game of kill or be killed. His dismissal of moral responsibility for the fates of Rosencrantz and Guildenstern with '*They* are not near my conscience' draws attention to what is – the King. 'Is't not perfect conscience/To quit him with this arm?' The issue of conscience is now like that of going to war with Hitler in 1939: 'is't not to be damn'd/ To let this canker of our nature come/In further evil?'. The reiteration of Claudius's crimes here (63-7) lays greater stress than before on them as crimes against the state of Denmark and the state of man ('our nature'), and on Hamlet as the agent deputed by Providence to excise the canker for the general good, regardless of consequences to himself. Nothing could be further from Laertes' narrow code of personal revenge. The dignified confidence to which Hamlet's speech moves swings sympathy to his cause, balancing his ruthless treatment of his schoolfellows.

Through Hamlet's regret 'that to Laertes I forgot myself' the narrative modulates to a reminder of the coming fencing match. His present control contrasts with his lapse into 'tow'ring passion'. His generous feelings towards Laertes contrast with Laertes' treachery. His perception of Laertes as a brother revenger –'by the image of my cause I see/The portraiture of his' – contains the dramatic irony of himself as revenge's object.

The entry of the fantastical courtier Osric lightens the undercurrent of mounting tragedy: Hamlet on top of his satirical form punctures, for the last time, the pretentiousness he hates. His contemptuous animal imagery (82-9) – 'water-fly', 'chuff' – introduces the fop as a brightly-coloured superficial chatterer well-suited to the bestial court he serves. We are alerted that in his ironical role he is doubly dangerous. Hamlet cannot take seriously such a sitting target for comic satire, yet, as we well know, he is in this incongruous disguise an innocent messenger of death. With all his laughable pretentiousness he yet works, with more skill than the King's previous tools displayed, on the weaknesses (or virtues?) Hamlet shares with Laertes: pride in the skills expected of 'an absolute gentleman', and concern for his honour. The challenge, set up (like the King's to Laertes) by praise of another's skill (anticipated in IV.vii.130–2) moves through the King's wager to the climax, with Hamlet in his contempt for the messenger completely off his guard, in the plain challenge to his honour, asking 'the opposition of your person in trial'. The 'water-fly' has caught the Prince – a life-like absurdity.

Hamlet's decision, for which Shakespeare has kept us in suspense through his delaying tactics and Osric's verbiage, is the courteous acceptance of a gentleman. Its repetition develops, for the audience, the dovetailing of Hamlet's 'purposes' with 'the King's pleasure' in the overruling design of a beneficent power. The Queen's message desiring him (as we know he already intends) to conciliate Laertes, renews interest in what form the overture will take, how Laertes will respond, and an irrational hope, whether it will disarm him. Swings between hope and fear mark the dramatic tension to the catastrophe.

Horatio's constant presence in V.ii as Hamlet's friend and confidant, second in the fencing match, and survivor trusted to report him and his cause 'aright', affirms, amid the treachery you know of, the values of love and loyalty; and enables Hamlet in turn to affirm to a sympathetic ear his faith in the inscrutable purposes of Providence. Horatio's normal soberness is lightened in the Osric episode when he joins modestly in the fun (129, 152, 183), though his plea for plain language (125) still asserts his commonsense. It is his simple responses, prompted by deep affection, which set up the opportunity for Hamlet's serene statement of the wisdom life has taught him about his role and meaning as he goes into the action which you know holds promise of death. Horatio's advice to Hamlet to obey his premonition 'how ill all's here about my heart', backing up the audience's knowledge of the King's plot with a powerful foreboding, gives added weight to Hamlet's noble valedictory acceptance of his mortal destiny, in his last intimate moments alone with Horatio (215–20):

We defy augury. There is special providence in the fall of a sparrow. If it be now, 'tis not to come; if it be not to come, it will be now; it if be not now, yet it will come. The readiness is all.

The tragic hero recognises a knowledge that, however long he lives, however deeply he studies men and the world, must be beyond him: 'Since no man, of aught he leaves, knows aught, what is't to leave betimes?' Yet against that ignorance he now knows his true purpose in life, to submit his will to an inscrutable Providence, ready to live or die as it directs.

The moral stature of Hamlet indicated in this interlude stays in your mind while you watch the organisation of the ceremony as a full-scale 'show' directed by the King, reminding you of the canker Hamlet must excise. The King's central control, embodied in the ritual, is mere appearance, demonstrated in his ironical role as peacemaker: 'Come, Hamlet, come, and take this hand from me'. For the audience, moral kingship resides in 'Hamlet the Dane', displaying the nobility, frankness, and generosity that make him vulnerable: the Prince Ophelia knew, integrated with the society he embraced as his rightful kingdom at Ophelia's grave. Shakespeare takes care, as his hero is about to lose his life, to make us regret the tragic waste of its worth.

The 'reconciliation' of Hamlet and Laertes (222-48) offers an ironic prelude to the treacherous revenge it conceals. Though Laertes' vow that he 'will not wrong' Hamlet's love can hardly be sincere now, this ritual of reconciliation foreshadows Laertes' repentance and their mutual forgiveness. Hamlet is neither insincere nor unjustified in excusing as his 'madness' the wrongs he has done Laertes' family. Only in part 'put on', it has included baser drives alien to his nobler self, bouts of instability, and the ungovernable frenzy in which he killed Polonius. His 'disclaiming from a *purpos'd* evil' honestly shows the limits to which his self-knowledge will take him. Hamlet's apology affirms a sense of himself as noble, despite bestial lapses: a sense of what he *is* being one of the few positives left to Shakespeare's tragic hero when simplified codes and systems cannot cope with complexity. Laertes' reply is based on the simplified code of honour idealising revenge. While our knowledge of the murder plot checks sympathy for Laertes, the speech shows a certain honesty in his admission that while he will not forego his revenge (unless advised by experts in honour) he will not act from malice, but to keep his name 'ungor'd'. This concern for reputation anticipates Hamlet's not to leave a 'wounded name' behind him.

From here to the end of the match (309) Shakespeare exploits the discrepancies of awareness between stage audience and theatre audience. Our anticipation aroused in IV.vii.128-47 is at first fulfilled: the stagecraft enacts the plot expounded there. Hamlet does not 'peruse the foils'. Laertes manufactures an excuse for making a second choice – which we know is the unblunted weapon. While Laertes 'anoints' it, the King's speech as Master of Ceremonies (264-75) focuses all eyes but yours. It draws your attention to the 'stoups of wine' and the 'cup' which will trace out, with the unbated sword, the Providential design that utilises and overrules the King's.

The conduct of the match, played in tense silence but for the laconic interjections belonging to it, provides the main action to the catastrophe. The theatrical tension of a skilled performance, already heightened by the epic Hollywood accompaniment of kettledrum, trumpet, and cannon, is further intensified through alternations of hope and fear: fear in every thrust of the poisoned sword, hope in Hamlet's refusals of the poisoned drink and his success in the first two bouts; until the irrational hope that he will escape is ended by the fatal wound.

The bouts are resonant with human purposes in conflict; the intervals belong to 'Heaven ordinant'. Hamlet's first rejection of the drink is a hitch in Claudius's plan; on his second refusal, Gertrude's unanticipated drinking is an 'end' 'none of [Claudius's] own'. 'Nothing neither way', implying some check in the third bout, such as a lock of weapons, gives Laertes the chance to attack Hamlet – 'Have at you now' – without the usual ritual warning 'Come (on)', inflict the fatal wound, and in turn receive his own when, in the *'scuffling'* precipitated by an 'incens'd' Hamlet's realisation that Laertes' sword is unblunted, *'they change rapiers'*. Yet the Providential design, clear in the stage movements, is woven by human character. Hamlet's disapproval of his uncle's drinking habits as well as his uncle (I.iv.15–20) prepares for his refusal to join him in the celebratory drink: Gertrude's light-hearted invitation to join her in the pledge instead is motivated by the love that takes her from the King's side to her son's where the wine has been sent. In Gertrude's last tender gesture of normal life, 'Come, let me wipe thy face', her impending death is counterpoised by the love she lives for (IV.vii.11–12): mother and son now seen in the *right* relationship (reversed in III.iv. by their estrangement). For a split second the 'accident' gives Claudius a chance to save his Queen at the cost of his safety and reputation. He does not. Self-preservation, not love, concerns him most.

We are as surprised as Hamlet by Laertes' sudden, and successful, lunge. The fatal wound, revealing to Hamlet the treachery of the unbated sword but not yet its poison, leads to the scuffling (Laertes naturally anxious to retain the poisoned weapon) and the exchange on which the catastrophe turns; and which, in giving Laertes his own death wound, shows him in a visible stage image 'justly kill'd with [his] own treachery' (313).

The frenetic tempo of the contest gives place to a stillness in which the truths enunciated before the 'audience to this act' (340) turn a deed of private vengeance into one of public justice and moral cleansing. But you are left in suspense for the King's doom while the Queen's refutation of her husband's lie with her last gasps, 'No, no, the drink, the drink! O my dear Hamlet!/The drink, the drink! I am poison'd' (315), and Laertes' confession (319–26) point one way: 'The King – the King's to blame'. Laertes directs you to the recoil pattern as Hamlet kills the King with his own and his agent's poisons providentially put into his hand.

Laertes' exchange of forgiveness with Hamlet (334–7) brings a new tone to the end of the play, restoring the brotherhood in which both are 'noble' and both tainted with the evil they would destroy; the guilt of each punished with death by the other. The 'treachery' Hamlet would 'seek . . . out' is within, Laertes asserts: 'It is here, Hamlet' – in human nature as well as 'the treacherous instrument' in his hand. Two persistent images, here realised on stage, of prison and poison, stress the guilt Hamlet shares with all human sinners; the 'canker' he cannot root out until his own death kills the bestial part of his own nature. The dual nature of revenge as duty and crime is revealed in the stage picture of Hamlet dying as both revenger and object of revenge. But Hamlet, though acknowledging the 'dram of evil' in himself, is not reconciled to Evil as Claudius is. Hamlet's bitter pun, 'Is thy union here?/Follow my mother' recalls the infection of Gertrude by her marriage which prompted Hamlet's own tragic sense of 'sullied flesh' and its sequel in Ophelia's madness and death. The journey of poisoned foil and cup across the stage is a visual emblem of the spread of evil contagion from Claudius to all who came into contact with him, and its final return to its source. Horatio, the cup snatched from him by Hamlet, is the only one to escape infection. His fitness is thus established to take temporary charge after Hamlet's death. Hamlet bequeaths to Fortinbras the fallen world he has rescued; for Fortinbras, like King Hamlet, gives the world 'assurance of a *man*'.

The guilt Hamlet no longer wishes to escape is dramatised in his command 'Let the door be lock'd', turning the stage into a prison for his murderous execution, and in his image of 'this fell sergeant Death'. The limitations of sullied flesh, once resented as a 'prison' for his 'infinite' faculties, now confirm the kind of achievements possible to a human will guided by an inscrutable but trustworthy Providence in the brief 'interim' revealed by Laertes to be 'not half an hour's life' (321). Practical considerations dominate Hamlet's interim: arrangements for the succession, and the reputation that will survive him. All his intense study has not plucked out the heart of the world's mystery, nor his own. But limited achievements for the on-going life process he once hated, not going beyond his role as partner of Providence, make Hamlet meaningful in the all-embracing but mysterious design: 'the rest is silence' (363). True to the dual face of existence he has come to recognise, Hamlet dies on a pun.

Most nineteenth-century productions ended the play with Hamlet's last words. But in the coda, Horatio, Fortinbras and the English ambassadors join to celebrate the many-sided meaning of Hamlet's life as friend, student, potential king, hero, and actor of roles. Preparing to switch our attention to them, two dramatic surprises shatter the stillness: the staid Horatio's passionate bid to die with his friend, and the 'warlike volley' offstage (357) with which Fortinbras 'with conquest come from Poland' greets the simultaneous arrival of the ambassadors from England. Authority is shared between the two men who speak for Hamlet the complete Renaissance prince, active and contemplative: Horatio the close friend, fellow-student, observer and interpreter; Fortinbras, whose armour, like the Ghost's, speaks of the duties of active commitment, to which Hamlet's life was sacrificed. The ambassadors may appear to be an anticlimax, but they are not superfluous. Among other functions their reminder of court ceremony attending on ambassadors (I.ii, II.ii) makes them a fit audience for the final ritual restoring order to Denmark, Hamlet's funeral procession.

Horatio plays both a private and a public role. His anguish as Hamlet's friend finds moving expression in his attempted suicide. His presence affirms the existence of noble human qualities which Hamlet could reveal only to him: love, innocence, conscience, honour, concern for truth.

The war-like drums of Fortinbras introduce a contrasting perspective on the 'sweet Prince' of Horatio's elegy (364-5) consigned to 'flights of angels'. You compare their victories as those of men committed to act from a sense of honour. Fortinbras's conclusion that the sight becomes the battlefield, reminds you of Hamlet's final acceptance of the soldier's role, to kill and be killed.

Remarkably, Fortinbras's elegy (complementary to Horatio's) celebrates human unfulfilment – which most of us can celebrate. Tragic exaltation lies in the heroic endeavour of a man who was never a soldier or a king to fulfil rightly the role life imposes on him in a deceptive world, with every part of the good-and-evil 'nature' the Ghost appeals to, despite lapses caused by the 'dram of evil' infecting his 'noble substance'. The *'peal of ordnance'* which sends us out of the theatre, reverberating throughout from I.iv where it celebrated Hamlet's reluctant decision to stay in Claudius's sullied kingdom, salutes as hero

> a man who, after questioning the meaning of creation, comes to accept a design in it beyond our comprehending, and who therefore, after seeking to withdraw from life through an abhorrence of all that is ugly and vicious in it, is finally – though tragically, not until death approaches – content to live life as it is, able to acknowledge, in word and deed, 'The readiness is all'.   (Jenkins, Arden edn,p.159)

3 THEMES AND ISSUES

3.1 HUMAN NATURE: BETWEEN OPPOSITE POLES

The range is from god-like to bestial, 'Hyperion' to 'satyr', Hamlet's father and uncle as he sees them; from virginal Ophelia to Gertrude in her sexual fall; from the jester 'wont to set the table on a roar', affectionate play-fellow of the child Hamlet, to Yorick's skull. Man is 'the paragon of animals', yet he is 'this quintessence of dust'.

3.2 HUMAN CHOICE, AND THE 'PROVIDENCE WHICH SHAPES OUR ENDS'

Modern playgoers who do not share Shakespeare's belief in the power of Providence should be able to suspend their disbelief in order to recognise it as the strongest force in the play. 'Our thoughts are ours', but – with 'purposes mistook/Fall'n on th'inventors' heads – 'their ends none of our own'. When in Act V Hamlet has come to understand his human purpose as the junior partner in a co-operation with the divine will, and is ready ('the readiness is all') to act when Providence shapes the situation for action, he has accepted the human condition.

3.3 ACCEPTANCE OR REJECTION OF LIFE

Hamlet's passionate desire to reject life in and for a world unbearably contaminated ('things rank and gross in nature/Possess it merely') comes to a climax in his debate on 'To be or not to be' and the nunnery scene which follows. The soliloquy comes down in reluctant favour of 'To be' only out of fear that death may not mean 'not to be', but worse ills than 'those . . . we have'. A nunnery should be Ophelia's refuge. 'Why', Hamlet exclaims, 'wouldst thou be a breeder of sinners?' 'We will have no more marriages'.

3.4 SEX, LOVE, AND MARRIAGE

The marriage denied Ophelia is balanced against Gertrude's second, which should never have taken place. A sequel to adultery, it was not only 'o'erhasty' but according to Hamlet's and Elizabethan ideas of the prohibited degrees of kinship, incestuous: it has made Hamlet son of a mother who is her 'husband's brother's wife'. Sexual desire has blinded her to the abysmal inferiority of her second husband to her first. Disgust at sexuality in her generates in Hamlet an obsession that condemns all women as frail sex-objects; including, tragically, Ophelia, in his eyes a potential one since she shares their sexual attractiveness. He claims, truly, to have 'lov'd Ophelia' (V.i.264), but his love being poisoned by his obsession, he tortures her – as well as himself – rejecting her with cruelty in the nunnery scene and insulting her in the play scene.

Where neither sex nor betrayal is concerned, he is loving and warm-hearted. He loves his father and Horatio; recollects Yorick with affection; greets his schoolfellows as old friends, warmly welcomes the Players and ensures them the best of hospitality. Even with his captors the pirates, off-stage, he comes to an amicable arrangement.

The love theme extends to the family of Polonius. He who 'in . . . youth suffered much extremity for love' has, like Jephthah, 'a daughter' whom he loves 'passing well'. He seeks, though not very wisely, to take good parental care of her and her brother. Her love for him as well as for Hamlet drives her to madness and death; his son's love for him makes that son his avenger.

3.5 REVENGE

Love of fathers fires Laertes and Hamlet with hate of their killers, fuelling revenge. Unless, in *Hamlet*, you accept that revenge is indeed the hero's duty, the play will not work; but the duty is inseparable from guilt, which is unmistakable in the other avengers, Laertes and Pyrrhus, and even, while he proposes to be one, Fortinbras with his 'lawless resolutes'. Among Elizabethan opinions on revenge, some condemned and some approved it. Shakespeare's dramatisation takes both points of view, and qualifications of them, into account.

3.6 ORDER AND DISORDER

Revenge is Hamlet's duty, though not a plain one: Laertes, pursuing revenge, would 'dare damnation', breaching divinely-appointed order. Hamlet's revenge has for its ultimate end to 'set right' a 'time' that is 'out of joint'. Disorder is firmly marked from the start. The relief challenges the sentry instead of the sentry challenging him. 'Lawless resolutes' have been 'shark'd up' by Fortinbras to overthrow an international agreement; urgent prepar-ations to resist him do not 'divide the Sunday from the week'. The Ghost is first addressed as 'thou that usurp'st this time of night'. Its appearance is believed to bode 'some strange eruption to our state'. The cause will be revealed as Claudius's seduction of Gertrude, fratricide, regicide, and usurpation: disruptions of order which, with the incestuous and 'o'erhasty' marriage to which we see Hamlet's reaction in I.ii, initiate the tragedy. Disorder in a Shakespearean drama may have gone so far that what would otherwise itself offend against order can be a right response. So it is with Hamlet's prolonged mourning, despite the orthodoxy of the King's reproof; so when in the closet scene son physically forces mother to sit and suffer his reproaches; so of course in his final killing of the King.

The theme is repeated in a comic key as he baits Polonius, Rosencrantz and Guildenstern. Horatio, his balanced integrity affectionately charac- terised by Hamlet, does much to keep alive the contrasting norm of order, reasserted, though the cost is and has been tragic, at the conclusion. The accession of Fortinbras will restore it in the state; Hamlet's due place in men's regard will be assured by his tribute and Horatio's testimony, and in the eyes of Heaven is imaged in Horatio's valediction: 'flights of angels sing thee to thy rest'.

3.7 APPEARANCE AND REALITY

From your first encounter with him, Hamlet is himself disordered in his response to a disordered world; nor can he recover the sense of an ordered self – of his true identity, an identity he seeks with limited success in a series of soliloquies. Sufficient adjustment to outer reality and unriddling of his own inner reality elude him. It is ironical that he, sincerest of men, who 'know[s] not "seems"' should be constrained to put on an 'antic disposition'. Claudius 'smiles and smiles'; the reality of him is villain, yet one who harbours a conscience. Apparently at prayer, he is therefore spared by Hamlet, lest he be sent to Heaven; in reality, lacking practical penitence, he is failing to pray. Everywhere, reality lurks behind appearance, like the eavesdroppers when Hamlet supposes himself alone with Ophelia or Gertrude. The false friendship of Rosencrantz and Guildenstern he quickly sees through. In comic dialogue with Polonius, his satirical thrusts and 'pregnant' replies pass for the happinesses 'that often madness hits on'. Osric, the comic butt of his wit, is at the same time bearer of the fatal invitation to the fencing match.

Conspiracy requires concealment of real purposes. A girl, intent it seems on a book of devotion, is being used as a decoy; in a cup of wine the rich pearl, the 'union' Claudius purports to drop, is in fact poison. The fencing match, his culminating attack on Hamlet's life, and the play, Hamlet's crucial attack on his conscience, are both deadly devices in the guise of recreation.

Hamlet returns to Denmark no longer disorientated towards either outer or inner reality. He can affirm his identity: he is 'Hamlet the Dane', who 'lov'd Ophelia'; in the world, he accepts that Providence, however inscrutable, is paramount, and will govern the fulfilment of his task.

4 TECHNICAL FEATURES

4.1 A NOTE ON DRAMATIC CONVENTIONS

A convention, in drama, is something the dramatist is taking for granted and which the audience agrees not to question: to begin with, that the actor Richard Burbage, or Derek Jacobi, is Hamlet. On television we are accustomed to plays which look and sound as if they were recorded from actual life (though by a well-understood convention the recording is not continuous: it 'cuts' from one sequence to another). Shakespeare's plays do not aim at literal resemblance to real life. In appreciating *Hamlet* we have to adjust to conventions which are not 'naturalistic'. On real-life assumptions, questions would be quite fair which in *Hamlet* should never occur to you: for instance, if there was an eye-witness who was able to describe Ophelia's drowning, why did he not go to the rescue? In Shakespearean drama, disregard of logic such as this is not a fault; it will not affect the audience, and Shakespeare's art cares only for what will.

4.2 CHARACTERS AND THEIR FUNCTIONS

In order to study character and Shakespeare's methods of characterisation, you should, as an actor would who has been offered a part, collect evidence from what each character says about himself, what others say about him, what he does when he is speaking, and when he is silent. Such an examination of words and actions in the context of what they build on and prepare for should illuminate the sub-text – the motives which lie beneath the actual words.

Characters

Hamlet
When you meet Hamlet he is not his normal self as recalled by Ophelia (III.i.151–6). The shock of his mother's 'o'erhasty' and incestuous re-

marriage to her late husband's brother, the 'bestial' uncle that Hamlet despises in comparison with his 'godlike' father, has plunged him in such deep melancholy that he wishes he need not go on living in so corrupt a world. When he is told by the Ghost that this uncle murdered his father, having made an adulteress of his mother, the shock is redoubled. He loves his father and already hates Claudius. Beneath his paralysing melancholy there lives the man of action Ophelia remembers; his first response is the vow to 'sweep to [his] revenge'. But his mind is almost unhinged. He is saved from the madness which threatens but never overwhelms him by finding channels through which it can discharge itself – the 'wild and whirling words' of his return to his companions, the hysteria of the oath-swearing scene (I.v.118-90), and subsequently the 'antic disposition' he puts on as cover for his dangerous knowledge and purposed vengeance. He fails, however, to sweep to his revenge. He reproaches himself repeatedly with his delay, and though some of his self-accusations are false (despite II.ii.565-72, he is obviously no coward) this one is confirmed by the Ghost's reappearance 'to whet thy almost blunted purpose'. He delays partly because the shocks have numbed his will. He can act only on the spur of the moment, as when he kills Polonius – then he has no time for 'thinking too precisely on th' event'. One result of his thinking, not to his discredit, is a questioning of the Ghost's word and its identity. He scruples to act until he is certain of the truth. This shows his strong sense of responsibility. That and his patriotism, since 'the time is out of joint' in Denmark, compel him to acknowledge, however reluctantly, his obligation to 'set it right'.

Revulsion from the blend of evil and good inescapable in human experience and personality is one of Hamlet's ruling characteristics. For him his father and uncle represent, without qualification, the godlike and bestial in human nature. There is truth in the contrast. Yet, unconscious of the inconsistencies, he assumes correctly that Claudius has a conscience the play scene will catch, and accepts that his father died an unabsolved sinner. The evil he feels in himself, his inheritance as a man and in particular as the son of a guilty mother, is something he cannot come to terms with. He is convinced it is a guilt that he and Ophelia must not pass on – does she want to be 'a breeder of sinners'?

His belief that unless she enters a nunnery she will go the way his mother has gone springs from another ruling characteristic. He is prone not only to reflect but to generalise. He generalises from the corruption he sees to a world totally spoiled by corruption. Gertrude's provokes the generalisation, 'Frailty, thy name is woman'. Though Ophelia has not yet succumbed to that frailty, he thinks she inevitably will. Hamlet loves her (V.i.264), but to his obsessive revulsion from sex and the propagation of sinful mankind, she is the temptress who would involve him in those contaminations, so he savages both his love and Ophelia.

That cruelty is part of the evil his character is not free from, and it is seen also in his callous indifference to the fate, half-justified though it may be, of his former schoolfellows and in the ferocity that possesses him from the intoxicating success of the play scene to the killing of Polonius and prompts his sparing the King at prayer to await an opportunity of sending him to Hell.

But the drams of evil do not call in question his essential nobility. He is all a Renaissance Prince should be: gifted and trained as courtier, soldier, scholar, concerned for his country, and for his personal honour; an athlete, a man of taste, a judge of plays and acting. He is courageous in following the Ghost and boarding the pirate, too generous to 'peruse the foils'. His scrupulous anxiety to do right is one of the traits which distinguishes him from the stock revenger. His own nobility is reflected in his conceptions of Laertes (V.i.217, V.ii.77-8), of Fortinbras (IV.iv.48-53) and of his father. The people and Horatio love him. He is endeared to us by his capacity for love both as a son, and towards Ophelia, even when it goes wrong; by his affection for Horatio and the memory of Yorick, and by the good terms on which he entertains the Players and talks with the Gravedigger. In his wit and humour, the breadth of his mind, his quests for the truth of his own nature, and the order of the universe, Hamlet is given something of Shakespeare's own genius.

Thanks principally to Hamlet's experience on the voyage, but assisted by his observation of Fortinbras's army, his character develops. The Prince who returns to Denmark can lay claim to his royal identity – 'I, Hamlet the Dane' – and his love of Ophelia. There is a new balance in his attitude to death and to life. He is reconciled not to evil but to its inescapable mingling with good, to the guilty duty of his role as avenger, and to the requisite co-operation in fulfilling it between his initiative and the Providence which he can trust to provide the opportunity.

Claudius

Claudius is not the despicable creature Hamlet depicts. He is skilled in role-playing, not least as King (though a drunkard), and in statecraft. He commands himself, it seems, during the dumb-show, and shows cool courage in face of Laertes' rebellion. But his abilities are no less conspicuous in manipulating his tools against Hamlet and contriving his death. He is an adulterous seducer, an incestuous husband and twice a poisoner, yet not without the complication of a conscience. His conscience is ineffective however against his overruling determination to preserve his gains and himself. Recognising that repentance is not for him, he is troubled by it no more.

Gertrude

Gertrude's conscience, awakened, does result in some development of character, so that Hamlet's trust in her is not misplaced. She loves her son, and in her way, Claudius, and is brave where she loves. She is good-natured though facile and sensual.

Ophelia

Ophelia's virgin purity is contrasted with Gertrude's sensuality and guilt. Innocent, not ignorant, a dutiful daughter, she has more spirit than is always recognised, as when she answers her brother's admonition with hers, and quietly stands up to Hamlet in the nunnery scene and play scene. Pathetic in her wounded love bravely borne, and in her madness, she then unconsciously reveals her preoccupations with her father, lover, and fantasies of sexual fulfilment.

Laertes

Laertes is a loving son and brother. Anguish at Ophelia's plight and grief at her death heighten his passionate determination to avenge his father's murder. In contrast with Hamlet he is the stock type of avenger, reckless and ruthless, all the more when he has succumbed to Claudius's suggestion of the treacherous means to employ and even bettered the instruction. Yet he takes pride in his honour as a gentleman, is not so free of scruple as he imagined, and by his repentant exchange of forgiveness with his victim, shows himself not devoid of the nobility Hamlet attributed to him.

Polonius

Polonius is a caring father but judges love and lovers, like all other situations and people, by worldly and stereotyped formulas. A busybody, fond of devious plans, he resorts once too often to spying. Neither at home nor as experienced adviser to Claudius is he a buffoon, though as garrulous wiseacre and Hamlet's butt he is often a comic figure.

Rosencrantz and Guildenstern, Osric, the Gravedigger

The role of the Fool or Clown is distributed among several characters. Polonius shares in it; Hamlet plays the fool, and makes fools of his two schoolfellows – who have one sycophantic personality between them – and of Osric, a brilliant thumb-nail sketch. The Gravedigger, a low-comedy figure, has a robust attitude to death, and in his dialogue with Hamlet gives as good as he gets.

Horatio, Fortinbras

Horatio, the true 'schoolfellow' contrasting the false ones, is exactly the stable character Hamlet would trust, and assuredly can. His courage is demonstrated in his confrontation of the Ghost (I.i). Heroically attempting to die with his friend, he is constrained to live and do him better service. Fortinbras, man of action, developed from lawless would-be revenger to conquering royal general will fitly rule the Denmark Hamlet has cleansed.

Functions

No characters have more vitality than Shakespeare's, and their vitality is most often convincingly life-like. Yet the play does not exist in order to

portray characters of seeming flesh and blood; the characters are called
into existence to enact the play. They have functions to perform as con-
tributions to it. Generally function and personality go hand in hand.
Nothing could be more in character than for the busybody Polonius,
meddling once too often, to provide the victim required in order that
Hamlet may become in his turn a murderer pursued by revenge. It is not,
however, personally characteristic of Gertrude that she describes, and so
poetically, Ophelia's death. The Queen's performance of the 'messenger'
role is not designed to illustrate her character, but to place dramatic stress
on the connection between Ophelia and Gertrude.

For the most part, minor personages (even the Players) simply behave
according to their functions. Shakespeare always defines both the person-
alities and the functions of his characters by the way he groups them. An
idea of the grouping in *Hamlet* can be given by a diagram. Hamlet and
Claudius are protagonist and antagonist; with Gertrude and the Ghost they
form a guilt-laden family. Hamlet is paired in no less mortal opposition
with Laertes, and in a doomed love-relationship with Ophelia. Their father,

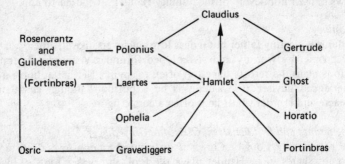

who completes the second family of the play, is killed by him, and, with
Ophelia, avenged by Laertes. Hamlet, Laertes, and (as at first conceived)
Fortinbras, each seek vengeance for a father: Hamlet and Laertes achieve
it, at the cost of killing each other. It was Horatio, Hamlet's valued friend
of Wittenberg days, who having seen the Ghost, brought Hamlet where he
could learn its message; and who remained his one confidant and ally,
surviving, with Fortinbras (earlier a contrasting foil to the Prince), to speak
his epitaph and do him final honour. The courtiers, Polonius, Rosencrantz
and Guildenstern, and Osric, are all baited by Hamlet. In provoking
laughter, they group themselves with the Gravediggers, who, however, as
cross-talk comedians, bring in a different kind of humour. Hamlet's
dialogue with the First Gravedigger is followed by his discovery that the
grave is to be Ophelia's.

Hamlet, then, is central in relation to every group and individual. All
these links and groupings are indicated in the diagram, but not the matching
of the two contrasted women, Ophelia and Gertrude. Groups and pairs,
like this one, have linkings of their own, not merely through Hamlet.

Character grouping has an important share in that part of Shakespeare's dramatic structure which consists of comparisons we are invited to make between things significantly alike, or significantly different.

4.3 STRUCTURE

Analysis of the play's structure yields the means by which the dramatist relates the parts of the play to each other and to the whole to bring out its central issues. Shakespeare builds *Hamlet* as a sequence of cause-and-effect, the plot; and also as a pattern of features that correspond, which can be called the symmetric structure. The plot provides the dynamic structure, generating the forward drive of the play. Not all the progression is in plot; the display of character can progress. New aspects may be revealed in an unchanged personality, as in Polonius at home, Polonius with the King; or the personality may develop in response to experience.

Dynamic structure
It is chiefly by the plot that the excitement is created which seizes and holds the attention of the audience. The plans the adversaries lay are all made known to us before they are put into practice, so that we await the outcome in suspense. What will the Ghost's message be when at last he speaks? Is the 'Mousetrap' going to work? In the fencing match will Hamlet after all survive?

The action is driven forward by cause and effect: it is up to us to notice the many connecting links. The revenge plot, the central series, is set going by Claudius's crimes. Revealed by the Ghost, they determine Hamlet's task, which prompts the antic disposition he puts on. One of them, by making Gertrude a mother who disgusts him, is a main cause of his paralysed delay. Her guilt is a causative factor in the Ophelia sub-plot. Projecting it onto Ophelia, Hamlet maltreats her in the nunnery scene and the play scene, confirming her in the belief that he is mad: and when the man she loves, in his 'madness' kills her father, her mind gives way, and 'incapable of her own distress', she drowns.

Drama depends on conflict. Alternate advances and set-backs for Hamlet make the dramatic conflict vivid. On the whole he gains ground, till this 'rising action' reaches its peak with his triumph in the play scene. Afterwards, in a 'falling action' from the killing of Polonius, with similar alternations, he loses it. Would you regard the turning-point, or crisis, as the prayer scene – an opportunity to fulfil his task such as never returns, though you can hardly wish him to have taken it? Or would you place it in the killing of Polonius?

Mastery of construction is seen further in Shakespeare's weaving together the various strands of his plot. Telling Claudius that Hamlet knows his secret, the play scene sets going the King's first counter-plot. The killing of Polonius provides him with public justification for sending the homicidal 'maniac' overseas. When Hamlet foils the secret design of having him put to death there, and returns to pursue the revenge which is his duty, the same killing, with in addition its effect on Ophelia, enables the King to enlist Laertes in his doubly murderous second counter-plot of the unbated foil and poisoned wine, to which he himself also falls victim, so that in his slaughter at Hamlet's hands, the original revenge plot is carried to its due conclusion. The envenoming of the foil, Laertes's embellishment of the King's plan, is similarly the cause of *his* death. The deaths of Polonius and of Rosencrantz and Guildenstern are also 'purposes mistook/Fall'n on th'inventors' heads'. The pair paid the price, though the 'inventor' of their mission was the King, of their misguided eagerness to earn his favour. Hamlet's 'Mousetrap', though successful in its purpose, alerts Claudius. In killing Polonius, his purpose went astray with fatal consequences. Accident dovetails with purpose, however. The chance encounter with the pirate ship coupled with Hamlet's forward valour, renews his opportunity to perform his task. Laertes' chance witnessing of Ophelia's piteous behaviour helps Claudius to whet him against Hamlet. After Hamlet has his death wound, the exchange of rapiers '*in scuffling*' catches Laertes in his own springe.

As the play moves to its conclusion all the strands of the plot are brought together. Beginning with Ophelia's burial, her drowning and her virginal sweetness are recalled. Hamlet avows his love: no other justice can be rendered her now. In the catastrophe accident and design work together to ensure justice. Gertrude's union with Claudius is ended by Claudius's 'union'. Claudius has a momentary choice of exposing his treachery or letting her die; his inaction does not prevent her warning cry to Hamlet. He sees the poisoned foil ensure the destruction of his brother's potential avenger; only for the vengeance, in consequence, to catch up with him. For revenges accomplished, Hamlet and Laertes pay with their lives, exchanging forgiveness. Fortinbras, returning a victor, honours Hamlet, and will restore order to a Denmark purged of Claudius.

Symmetric structure

The play is enriched by its symmetric structure of correspondences. In the theatre much cross-referring happens subconsciously. Studying the pages at leisure, you can look out for the correspondences with attention. Hamlet with sword suspended over King Claudius is prefigured by Pyrrhus with his suspended over King Priam; Ophelia's real madness by her lament over what she takes to be Hamlet's. Correspondences of primary importance leap to the eye. The crime from which the whole revenge action springs is presented three times; narrated by the Ghost, and staged in the dumb-show and again in the play it introduced. The Ghost reappears to Hamlet in his mother's closet. Shakespeare is fond of scenes which in mid-play remind you of early ones: in other plays they mark how far the action has moved; here, how far it has not.

Central to the drama and its meaning is the parallel, emphasised repeatedly, of Hamlet and Laertes, sons who revenge their fathers while suffering revenge they have provoked. The legendary Pyrrhus also avenges a father, and Fortinbras was setting out to do so when you first heard of him. In Laertes and Pyrrhus are depicted the sort of avenger Hamlet might have been but was not, though a touch of their quality is seen in him after the play-scene, and in his reason for sparing the King and his callous indifference over the fate of Rosencrantz and Guildenstern. In action and speech Laertes is a revenger without scruple: point-by-point comparisons show Hamlet to be the opposite. For example, Laertes begins by accusing the King of a responsibility for Polonius's death of which he is guiltless: Hamlet took care, before renewing his commitment to vengeance, to verify Claudius's guilt. For Hamlet there is a 'relish of salvation' in even a Claudius at prayer: Laertes would cut Hamlet's throat 'i'th'church' and 'dare damnation'.

Patterns of correspondence are to be traced in all the kinds of feature which go to make up the play. Among characters, Hamlet is always comparing his uncle with his father. Gertrude, guilty and sensual, is the antitype of Ophelia, virginal and innocent. Hamlet has a foil in Fortinbras. There are comparable types of scene: scenes where Hamlet baits Polonius, or Rosencrantz and Guildenstern, or Osric; or scenes where the stage is full, with the King and Queen enthroned – the Council scene, the play scene, the fencing match. The spying motif has been introduced in the Reynaldo scene before being raised to a higher power in the two eavesdropping scenes.

Some phrases call up mental pictures (imagery) and when the images remind us of each other, they form part of the symmetric structure. Caroline Spurgeon (*Shakespeare's Imagery and What it Tells us*, New York, 1935) identified a dominant image in *Hamlet*, that of an ulcer or tumour which mines inwardly; an image of the rotten state of Denmark. The motif of Hamlet's paralysing revulsion from the stains of living and procreating has a recurrent image picturing vile fertility. For the theatre audience, the stage properties are images physically visible. A number resemble each other in being made the occasion of commentary by Hamlet: the recorder, the miniatures of his father and uncle, Yorick's skull. Somewhat similarly, Ophelia's flowers are eloquent in the appropriateness with which she bestows them.

4.4 STYLE

The verse: introduction and survey

This spirit, dumb to us, will speak to him.
    u -/u   - /u - / u   - /u - /

This is a line whose rhythm agrees exactly with the basic norm (the 'metre') of Shakespeare's dramatic verse. It has five beats: that is, it has in it five syllables we stress when we speak it. The five units, each containing one of them, are each in 'rising rhythm', an unstressed syllable followed by a stressed one: u - (an 'iambic foot'). The five iambic feet make up an 'iambic pentameter'. The lines ('blank verse') do not rhyme.

If all the lines were of exactly this pattern the verse would be unbearably monotonous. In *Hamlet* it is very flexible. The variations are governed by the way it is natural to speak the lines according to the meanings and emotions they express. Enough lines follow the norm, and practically all come close enough to it, to establish it as what the ear expects. That expectation is either fulfilled, or pleasurably disappointed in an appropriate way, when they are spoken as sentences, exclamations or the like. In the above example the sentence rhythm exactly fits the expected rhythm of the verse: 'dumb' and 'speak' are words which would always carry a stress, but most often 'us' and 'him' would not: it is because they are being contrasted that they, even more than the other contrasted pair, are said with emphasis: 'dumb to *us*, will speak to *him*. In

O horrible! O horrible! most horrible!
u - /u u /u - /u u   - / - u u /

the established rhythm is violently departed from to express the Ghost's violent emotion and the offence against nature he is describing. The line has only four stresses; but three are of fearful power, and the last of these comes straight after the previous stress without a light syllable between: two light syllables complete the line, instead of a light one and a stress. A milder example reports Hamlet's distraught intrusion on Ophelia:

Pale as his shirt, his knees knocking each other,
- u/u   - /u   - / - u /u - u /

where two stresses knock against each other, like Hamlet's knees, the first foot is 'reversed', beginning instead of ending with its stress (on 'Pale'), and the line has a light syllable extra (a 'feminine ending'). These last two variations Shakespeare continually employs, sometimes for a special effect of meaning or feeling (the Ghost emphatically is *'Doom'd* for a certain term') but often led simply by his never-failing ear for the tones of the speaking voice, for him the voice of the actor speaking the lines 'trippingly on the tongue'. That movement depends greatly on the varied positions of the pauses (always worth your notice). In some of the speeches, especially the big ones, lines of less than full length are used at appropriate points, to denote a turn of thought, as with Hamlet's 'Yet I', in his 'O what a rogue' soliloquy. Many of Shakespeare's lines have only four stresses: for example

He's lov'd of the distracted multitude;
-   /u u /u - /u   - /u-   /

where your sense of the accustomed rhythm persuades your ear to accept a light syllable ('the') in the place of one of the regular five.

A speaker sometimes ends with a part-line; if another replies, usually he completes it; but there are exceptions. As the closet scene begins, Hamlet and Gertrude speak in one-line retorts like those in Classical drama (*stichomythia*).

> QUEEN   Hamlet, thou hast thy father much offended.
> HAMLET   Mother, you have my father much offended.
> QUEEN   Come, come, you answer with an idle tongue.
> HAMLET   Go, go, you answer with a wicked tongue.

For the Pyrrhus recital and the *Gonzago* play, Shakespeare has to devise styles that will differentiate them from the dialogue of *Hamlet* proper. The blank verse of the Pyrrhus speech is heightened with hyperbole and 'high astounding terms' like Marlowe's. The *Gonzago* play is in rhymed couplets; and is elaborately artificial in style. Outside *Gonzago* there are no rhymed dialogues, but in most of the scenes which end in verse Shakespeare adopts the convention of a clinching rhymed couplet to round them off. The 'numbers' Hamlet owns himself 'ill at' in his love-letter are lines of three beats, not five: an epigram pivoted on the word 'doubt'. It is in rhyme, like the snatches of ballad-verse he quotes at Polonius or after the play-scene perhaps invents; and those bawdy or pious ones the mad Ophelia sings.

Shakespeare then, varies, or varies from, his staple blank verse; he is the master of his versification, not its slave. His greatest variation, of course, is between verse and prose.

Prose and verse

There is always a good dramatic reason why Shakespeare turns to prose. When, in *Hamlet*, does he use it? The rule-of-thumb explanations - for plebeians, for comedy, for minds so disordered (in reality, or pretence) that the ordered utterance of verse is beyond them - though they will take you some way, are insufficient. The Gravediggers are plebeians and comic; if Osric, one of the gentry, does not speak verse, it is because he is comic too. Ophelia speaks prose in her madness; but also in the play scene, where she is perfectly sane. Speaking it sanely with her there (though in his 'antic' role at first with the King), with Polonius, Rosencrantz and Guildenstern, the Prince is often both making fun of them, and playing the madman; but he speaks prose elsewhere outside that role: with the Players and sometimes with Horatio, for instance in the graveyard meditations upon death. The unfailing cue for prose and verse is the nature of the episode or its immediate neighbours. Francisco and Barnardo, ordinary honest soldiers, begin the play with verse, lending impulse and some dignity from the start, and in keeping with the Ghost episode so soon to come. In the play-scene all the aristocratic audience speak prose, to distinguish them firmly from the play in couplets. Between that scene and the one with Rosencrantz and Guildenstern which then follows, Hamlet and

Horatio do not shift back into verse (and prose suits well enough with the way Hamlet's success has gone to his head). When the Players – no aristo-crats – are not performing, prose is their element, and Hamlet joins them in it. In the nunnery scene, Ophelia talking with the 'mad' Hamlet, speaks it; but on his departure laments in verse. The Gravedigger determines the mode of Hamlet's dialogue with him; with Horatio, Hamlet continues in the same medium, making the sharper contrast when the burial procession enters. As always, Shakespeare's eye (or rather, ear) is on what will best serve the scene.

The nature of the prose

The prose does not imitate the casual negligence of conversation. It is as much an art-form as the verse: closely organised to furnish what the play requires. In a sustained passage like Hamlet's advice to the Players, the balanced phrases create a pattern as strong as the metrical lines do in the verse. In brief exchanges, a shape is created by the way the participants answer each other.

The language of *Hamlet*

(i) Kinds and characteristics

At times the language, like Francisco and Barnardo's, does give a more or less colloquial impression. The King's speech in the Council scene (I.ii) has all the formality of a public address. Official formality yields strong pattern, but so (of quite another kind) does emotion. You speak rhythmically when you are moved; as Ophelia does in her lament, and Hamlet frequently, as when balancing alternatives in the inner debate of 'To be or not to be'. Like his other soliloquies, this, for the actor, is a 'set speech'. Similarly Claudius, attempting to pray, has his: and Hamlet has others in prose: 'I have . . . lost all my mirth' (II.ii.295ff.), for example, culminating in 'What piece of work is a man . . .' A different kind of set speech is the narration – the Ghost's, or Horatio's retrospect (I.i.84–110). The report – Hamlet's of his voyage, the Queen's of Ophelia's death – is a particular form of this.

In contrast, there is quick-fire dialogue, as when Hamlet is running rings round Polonius or Rosencrantz and Guildenstern, or giving the Gravedigger as good as he gets. Repartee is a weapon in these encounters. Hamlet employs it also against the King, and retorts to Ophelia's 'Tis brief, my lord', 'As woman's love'.

Hamlet abounds in phrases often quoted because they have proved memorable for their wit, humour, pathos, or poetic power. Its diction and vocabulary are characterised by words plain and words coloured, not excluding the vulgar or bawdy. Hamlet's mind, so alive to language, is addicted to double meanings, bawdy when torturing Ophelia in the play-scene but often an acceptable means of attack and defence against the King and his tools. In *Hamlet* Shakespeare commands its whole range, including poetry of two distinct kinds. In such a phrase as Hamlet's asking why the Ghost, 'in complete steel/Revisits thus the glimpses of the moon', or in Horatio's lines about 'the morn in russet mantle clad', or in the Queen's report of Ophelia's drowning, a lyrical note is heard. But there is also poetry which is poetical in virtue of its dramatic intensity: 'this fell sergeant, Death,/Is strict in his arrest', or 'Absent thee from felicity awhile'. Indeed, simply as words, the words may be of the plainest: 'The readiness is all', 'The rest is silence'.

There are many characteristics of the expression to be noted. One is the pace and movement of the verse. Is it quick, vehement – the sense running on from line to line without pause ('enjambement'); or is it full of pauses, continually so at the ends of the lines ('end-stopped')? Are the phrases related in a simple way to each other? Or, as in 'To be or not to be', are they linked in an elaborate sequence? Or are they disjointed; as not only Ophelia's in her insanity are, but Hamlet's after returning from the Ghost, so that Horatio says 'These are but wild and whirling words, my lord', and of course when he puts on an 'antic disposition'? The meaning may be straightforward, but it may be ironic, and in more than one way. The words may be ironically intended by the speaker: 'Thrift, thrift, Horatio'. Or he may be relishing an irony in the situation: 'sport', when the 'enginer' is 'Hoist with his own petard'. Or there may be in his words an irony he is unaware of ('dramatic' or 'Sophoclean' irony). So it is with the Queen's hope that Ophelia's virtues may restore Hamlet, bringing honour to them both; and Polonius's belief that wisdom like his may be trusted 'by indirections' to 'find directions out', a policy which, applied to Hamlet, does not result as he expects.

While Hamlet mocks Polonius, or the twin catspaws, or Osric, the tone is comic; the Gravedigger and his 'feed' are a comic 'turn'; and Polonius makes himself a figure of fun when, announcing that 'brevity is the soul of wit', he persists in beating about the bush despite the Queen's demand for 'More matter with less art'. In other episodes the tone is of pathos. Ophelia, sane, knows her own misery, 'of ladies most deject and wretched', yet says more in pity of Hamlet than of herself. Mad, and 'incapable of her own distress', yet pitying her father laid 'in the cold ground', she moves you through her own plight, but also by how that moves the onlookers, as she turns 'affliction' to 'favour and to prettiness'. Contrasting both with the pathos and the comedy, the tone of other episodes is passionate with disgust, reproof, fury, or self-reproach.

Certain particular forms of expression are bound to catch your attention: questions, misunderstandings, and misinterpretations of words and phrases, puns of more than one kind. In his attempt to pray, Claudius has a mounting series of questions to ask of Heaven and of himself. In 'O what a rogue . . .' Hamlet puts to himself questions like 'Am I a coward?' For him they demand the answer 'yes', which the audience knows him rather better than to concur with. The debate with himself in 'To be or not to be' is conducted, naturally enough, as question and answer. Misunderstandings can be genuine (to comic effect): when Hamlet, unrecognised, asks 'Upon what ground' Hamlet lost his wits, the Gravedigger replies, 'Why, here in Denmark'. But Hamlet often gives a phrase a turn unintended by the speaker: 'Still better, and worse' - 'So you mis-take your husbands'; 'Will you walk out of the air, my lord?' - 'Into my grave?' Puns may be light-hearted, as when Hamlet puns, with 'a brute part' and 'so capital a calf' on Polonius's 'I was killed in the Capitol. Brutus killed me'. But in the first words of his conflict with Claudius, 'a little more than kin, and less than kind', the pun is bitter; and in almost the last it is savagely passionate: 'Is thy union here?'

It is not enough to recognise these features and kinds of style, and find words to describe them. Studying *Hamlet* will mean attempting to see and say how they help to build the play, and work on the audience to make it dramatic. You notice, of course, the vulgar expression 'lug the guts' (III.iv.214). But what, as drama, does it *do*? It shows, you reply, Hamlet's present state of mind, and indeed one strand in his character; and gives the stage business of his exit its full effect, as he drags the body unceremoniously with him.

(ii) Dramatic purposes

Among the dramatic purposes of language which recur is the simple one of giving information: about how things stand ('Situation') - Horatio brought by Marcellus to overcome his disbelief in the Ghost; about character - Hamlet on Horatio's; about character relationships - 'our sometime sister, now our Queen'. Another and related one is to describe what is not enacted: King Hamlet's murder, Ophelia's drowning, Hamlet's changing the death-warrant and the encounter with the pirate ship. The language itself enacts conflict, as when Hamlet resists the rebukes of his continued mourning, or Claudius, threatened by Laertes, stands firm; or you hear his and Hamlet's conflicts with themselves. The conflicts, given words, depict character. Characters are portrayed by what others say about them: from Ophelia, you learn what the normal Hamlet was like before the shocks which drove him to melancholy. They characterise themselves by what they say, but also by how they say it. Granville Barker (*Hamlet*, pp.182-6) observes the reflection in their styles of the instability of Gertrude and Laertes, distinguishes those of Claudius's private mind and his public utterance, and brilliantly analyses 'the tune' of Polonius and the variations in it which denote the garrulous old man who can lose the thread of his discourse; the wiseacre who is yet no babbling fool, the on-the-whole respected councillor; the careful, affectionate, if not very wise father; and, one may add, the man of maxims, who sees everything in terms of stereotypes.

Response to the characters on the part of the audience is guided by the language. It evokes sympathy for Ophelia, sane or mad; for Hamlet in the task which - 'O cursed spite!' - has fallen to his lot; in his repinings and self-reproaches, and his premonition of the end; and even for Polonius, Gertrude, and Claudius, of whom it prevents too simple a view. Polonius humbles himself to his child in confessing himself mistaken in his stereo-typed appraisal of Hamlet's courtship. Gertrude's remorse of conscience is movingly expressed. Claudius shows he is not devoid of it, and against the onslaught of Laertes bears himself as royally as if the throne were his by right. Response to Hamlet, likewise, is not permitted to be too simple. Sympathy is alienated from him when he exclaims 'Now could I drink hot blood', and by Horatio's troubled comment 'So Guildenstern and Rosencrantz go to't' where not even Hamlet's justification quite eclipses the vindictiveness of 'Not shriving-time allow'd'. But no qualification is suffered to make the audience question the rightness of its essential sympathy with Hamlet or alienation from Laertes and Claudius. As they are conspiring to murder him, the alienation is even reinforced by their scorn of the church and its privilege of sanctuary. In its presentation of the characters, constantly the language expresses their emotions: in 'I was the more deceived' Ophelia's wounded love, of necessity accepting its rejection; in 'Where is this King?' Laertes' rage and contempt. And on particular occasions it portrays a mental state: 'how ill all's here about my heart'; or even a physical one: 'Our son is fat [sweaty] and out of breath'.

To bring them repeatedly to attention, themes and issues are embodied in memorable words: 'Seems, madam? . . . I know not "seems" '; 'the time is out of joint', 'this . . . sullied flesh', 'almost blunted purpose', 'scourge and minister', 'there is a special providence in the fall of a sparrow'. The language calls up images, like Shakespeare's favourite for rebellion that swamps order: 'The ocean, overpeering of his list'. Repeated images – 'the ulcerous place', the 'unweeded garden' – and those which associate with them create a pattern throughout the play. Emphasis by pattern is a device of style employed also on the small scale. The pattern may consist in repetition: by Laertes and the Queen – 'Alas, then she is drown'd' – 'Drown'd, drown'd'. It may be alliterative: 'What's Hecuba to him or he to Hecuba?'; or a matter of rhythm: 'Remorseless, treacherous, lecherous, kindless villain!'

Shakespeare's command of style is what affords him his control over the progress of a speech, episode, or scene, as he varies to that end the movement of his verse, the structure of his sentences, the pauses in both; and chooses his words for both their sense and sound. By model analyses of Hamlet's soliloquy 'O what a rogue . . .', and of the episode where he greets Horatio and is told of the Ghost, Granville Barker (*Hamlet*, pp.188–95) demonstrates in detail how this incomparably flexible command of style operates, and the control it achieves.

It goes hand-in-hand with Shakespeare's other language as a dramatist: his non-verbal stagecraft. It interacts with what the audience sees, either by the style itself, or descriptively. At entries and exits, what is spoken focuses the attention of both stage-audience and theatre audience ('Look where it comes again') and may add significance: 'In the same figure as the King that's dead' identifies the apparition, and the awe in Barnardo's voice should make you share it. 'See, it stalks away' prescribes the actor's gait, and doubles verbally what he shows visually. In the closet scene, Hamlet's 'My father, in his habit as he liv'd' ensures notice of the changed costume; 'Look where he goes even now out at the portal' has the Queen staring towards it, and because you as well as Hamlet see him, emphasises her blindness, already made explicit by her 'all that is I see' (when your eyes testify that she does not). It is the cue, besides, for her 'This is the very coinage of your brain', and Hamlet's admonition 'Lay not that flattering unction to your soul'. Words co-operate with stage business when 'The King rises', and he and Polonius call for lights as he flees from the play-scene; and in 'Dead, for a ducat, dead!' and 'Let him go, Gertrude'. Hamlet puts down that most dramatic of stage properties, Yorick's skull, with 'Dost thou think Alexander . . . smelt so? Pah!' The audience cannot smell the skull, but Hamlet can, and his words go near to add a sense to their perception of it. If, as seems highly probable, Hamlet shows his mother two miniatures in the closet scene, the audience cannot see the contrasted likenesses, though it knows, and this is what matters, that Gertrude can. But the significance of the two 'props' is created by the antithesis Hamlet describes them showing, between god-like nobility and bestial deformity. Stage properties, stage business, entries and exits, with other resources of Elizabethan stage spectacle, unite with the dialogue in Shakespeare's language of dramatic art, the language *Hamlet* is written in.

4.5 STAGECRAFT

Shakespeare's expression of his design through means other than verbal statement is supremely important in *Hamlet*. Powerfully expressed by stage images, the central theme of Hamlet's dual role as avenger and victim of revenge neither receives nor needs much said of it by Hamlet himself. You see the revenger inviting revenge upon himself by killing Laertes' father, and reflections of his dual role in Lucianus and Pyrrhus. What you see on stage constitutes the truth you can set against misrepresentation. The *Gonzago* play and dumb-show, though fictional, re-enact the truth of King Hamlet's murder to give the lie to the 'forged process' of his death which held the ear of Denmark.

The parts Shakespeare wrote were tailored to the actors in his company. As his leading actor, Burbage, grew older, so did his roles. But catering for his individual actors, Shakespeare never failed to serve the purposes of the play. The Gravedigger's part, fitting Robert Armin's strain of intellectual comedy and his good singing voice, demonstrates a tuneful acceptance of mortality contrasting with Hamlet's disgust. The Elizabethan convention of using boys to play women's roles would add conviction to Ophelia's innocence.

Other dramatic conventions (for example, the 'Messenger') provide important 'turns' for minor characters. The convention ensures your attention to off-stage events vital to the plot – the madness of Ophelia, the rebellion of Laertes. Frustration of expected conventions is used to draw attention to a breach of order: the Ghost in unusual costume, the Prince lagging behind the Royal procession into Council, the son bidding his mother 'sit you down, you shall not budge'. The poisonings in dumb-show and play, Pyrrhus with sword upraised, Laertes demanding of Claudius vengeance for his father, are stock revenge-tragedy images, with which Hamlet, complex revenger dissecting the moral issues of his dual task, unexpectedly and therefore emphatically fails to conform.

Yet adherence to stage conventions provides many dramatic effects. Shakespeare is unlikely to have spoiled the dramatic irony of the nunnery scene by ignoring the stage convention for the audience, in eavesdropping scenes, always to know who is aware of whom. (See 6.1, 'Problems and Non-Problems', for theories that Hamlet was, or became aware of, the eavesdropping.) Shakespeare employs asides to create a bond (not always of sympathy) through knowledge shared. Consider Shakespeare's purposes in such confidences to the audience as Hamlet's 'A little more than kin, and less than kind', Polonius's 'Still harping on my daughter'. The soliloquy, also exploiting the actor's intimate relationship with audience in the Elizabethan theatre to take you into the speaker's unspoken thought, is vital to the presentation of a man isolated from the world he lives in.

The dramatic change from soliloquy to action or vice versa is aided by the theatre's freedom from realistic expectations. With little scenery the actor provided the focus. Grouped pictorially against the permanent facade of the tiring house, actors could stress the contrast between the 'prison' of Claudius's court and the limitless mental world of Hamlet's soliloquies, delivered directly to audience from the foot of the open stage. Where precise location is important it is indicated in the text: Polonius and Rosencrantz set the meeting of Hamlet and Gertrude in the Queen's closet, in spite of directors who place it in the bedroom. When King and Court depart at the end of I.ii the Council Chamber goes with them. The actors' response to their environment – their bearing, gestures, voices, costumes, stage properties – is Shakespeare's major means of changing the scene. The move from the cold ghost-haunted battlements of I.i to the Council Chamber of I.ii is accomplished by outside clothing being exchanged for resplendant Royal regalia; the nervy voices of the guards calling over misty spaces for the normally calm voice of Claudius giving his public address.

Without modern lighting, indications of time of day in the dialogue achieve a similar imaginative force. Hamlet's evocation, after the play scene, of the time when 'hell . . . breathes out/Contagion' expresses a blackness in his soul as well as the night. When necessary, precise time or passage of time is established: the ghost seen 'jump at this dead hour' is backed up by 'the bell then beating one'. But, as Granville Barker demonstrates (*Hamlet*, 39-44) Shakespeare makes use of the audience's acceptance of the elasticity of time both in stage convention and in subjective perception to measure it by the dramatic pulse rather than the clock. As plot and counter-plot rush to their conclusion references to precise time increase the tension. What matters, ultimately, is not how long or short a time

Hamlet has to live, but 'the interim is mine'. Playing without intervals gave an illusion of continuous action and emphasised comparison, contrast, and ironic juxtaposition of scenes. Otherwise the play would lose the dramatic effect of the cumulative contrasts of Ophelia's madness, the plotting of Laertes and the King, the humour of the Gravedigger and his 'feed', and Hamlet meditating on the jester's skull by the grave that levels all contrasts.

The size of Shakespeare's stage is one of its physical features that simplifies the audience's acceptance of non-naturalistic conventions. Its size easily separates actors for eavesdropping or asides; gives scope for the ceremonial, military or royal, which expands a few actors into Fortinbras's 'twenty thousand men' or Claudius's court; can accommodate a spectacle plus a full-stage audience, as in the play scene or the fencing match. On the other hand the emptiness of a large stage points the paradox of man's weakness and greatness as he fills it with soliloquy. It allows the Ghost to make an impressive entry and to 'stalk' away as majestically as the text requires. Its depth and width offer thematic perspectives. In V.i Hamlet and Horatio comment unobserved from a distance, until Hamlet speaks to the Gravedigger by the trap-door grave. When Ophelia's funeral procession enters from one of the tiring house doors, the depth of the stage gives them time to move away to become once more an unobserved audience as Ophelia's 'maimed rites' take centre stage. The vista of infinite space conjured up by the procession entering from the back ends in the constricted 'prison' of the grave – one of the paradoxes of the human condition that constantly exercises Hamlet's mind. Yet his leap into the grave at 'This is I, Hamlet the Dane' signals his full acceptance of the mortal condition.

The trap-door gives entry to the space under the stage associated with theatrical representations of Hell. That the Ghost made its entry through the trap is unlikely: a long 'stalk' seems implied by Horatio's 'Look, my lord, it comes'. But its use of the understage area for the swearing ritual indicates to the audience that Hamlet's duty of revenge is prompted by Hell as well as Heaven.

The discovery space provides cover for the eavesdroppers. The obscuring arras through which Hamlet stabs Polonius renders both their 'purposes mistook'. The two doors giving access from tiring house to stage strongly mark the limits of an episode, reinforcing contrasts and comparisons demonstrated by continuous playing. The exit of the martial Ghost through one door as the new King and court enter in full pomp from the other vividly contrasts their two worlds. A door focuses expectation of action that will change the situation. Doors are vital in the stagecraft by which Laertes' rebellion is dramatised. Claudius calling his Switzers to guard the door, the precipitate entry of the messenger reporting the rebellion, the mob uproar ('*within*'), the crash at 'the doors are broke', work up Laertes' stormy entry. Exits, especially when accompanied by such memorable clinching lines as 'The play's the thing/Wherein I'll catch the conscience of the King', keep excitement bubbling for fulfilment of their promise. Departure from an established pattern of entry and exit can imply change, as when from III.iii Shakespeare breaks and never fully re-establishes that of joint entries and exits by King and Queen. On a stage without a front curtain, actors had to give reasons for their exits – 'Come away', 'Break we our watch up'. Consider the way Shakespeare uses such utilitarian phrases to clinch the scenes they conclude. The necessity of removing dead bodies in full view gives Shakespeare occasion to dignify human beings with ritual, as when Hamlet's (unlike Polonius's) is given heroic status by the full military honours accorded him.

To this spectacle 'the soldier's music' adds an emotional dimension, as does the solemn bell announcing the approach of Ophelia's funeral procession. Theatre music is a dramatic shorthand well understood by the audience. Drums and cannon conjure up to the mind's ear Fortinbras's entire army. The loud aggressive music liked by Claudius and disliked by Hamlet suggests the King's brassy 'show' and rowdy behaviour of the drunken court. Contrasting with the depiction of Claudius's public face, the simple traditional music of Ophelia's ballads conveys a private emotion universalised in basic experiences of love, betrayal, and death.

The stage spectacle to which music adds emotional power includes movement, grouping, stage business, properties, costume. Costume is emblematic in a play whose hero probes for truth beneath outward appearance and discovers some basic truths to live by through assuming various roles. Hamlet's 'nighted colour', traditional garb of mourning and melancholy, sets him apart from both the showy court of Claudius and Fortinbras's soldiers. Costume change indicates change of role: the disordered dress expected of the distracted stage lover proclaims Hamlet mad to Polonius the dealer in stereotypes, but to the Globe audience, the actor of a role deliberately 'put on'. Untraditional stage costume, like the Ghost's armour and dressing gown, causes unease.

Stage properties carry symbolic concepts. To the Elizabethan audience, well versed in the language of flowers, Ophelia's distribution of flowers in IV.v indicates the moral order missing from Denmark. A recorder points the lesson to Rosencrantz and Guildenstern that they cannot play upon Hamlet. The devotional book given to colour Ophelia's presence in the lobby affords a trite moral to Polonius, a sharp sting to the King's conscience. The two miniatures of the brother kings make visual Hamlet's idealising tendency to keep good and evil separate: 'Look here upon this picture, and on this'. The sword raised over the praying Claudius focuses the brutal meaning of revenge. The poisoned foil and cup provide a helpful focus in V.ii for the audience to follow the interrelated dance of providential design, human planning, accident, and improvisation, which finally returns the poison infecting the kingdom to its source. The movements thus drawing the characters to their appointed end, with death hanging on every thrust of the poisoned foil, make the climactic stage spectacle a ritual of high tension. Most often in his scenes of spectacle (the Ghost, the play-scene, the fight in Ophelia's grave) Shakespeare encapsulates an image that marks a crisis.

5 DRAMATIC FORM:
HAMLET AS A TRAGEDY

> Shakespeare was not attempting to justify the ways of God to men . . .
> He was writing tragedy, and tragedy would not be tragedy if it were not
> a painful mystery.
>
> (A. C. Bradley, 1904)

For characteristics of Shakespearean tragedy see 'An Introduction to the
Study of Shakespeare's Plays', p.x.

5.1   *HAMLET* AS A TRAGEDY

Hamlet has the most prominent features of a tragedy, as Shakespeare and
many dramatists of his time evidently understood tragedy. It has a tragic
hero (protagonist) of high rank, on whom for his predominantly high
character our sympathies are principally centred, and who ends in a tragic
catastrophe which he has a decisive share in bringing about. He is confronted by a situation which is more than he can cope with until by tragic
errors in facing it he has helped to bring catastrophe on others as well as
himself: innocent, like Ophelia, or if, like Gertrude, Rosencrantz and
Guildenstern, Polonius, and even Laertes, they are chief authors of their
own disasters, not fully deserving what happens to them. *Hamlet* is tragedy
because the want of poetic justice, for them and the hero, keeps it a
painful mystery; and because the chain of cause and effect prevents it
equally from being 'Absurd' drama, as does Hamlet's final acceptance of
Providence at work in it to 'shape our ends'.

5.2   HAMLET AS TRAGIC HERO

What is there about Hamlet that makes him vulnerable to tragedy? We will
not find the answer in some single 'tragic flaw'. Start from Hamlet's tragic
errors, and then ask what traits of character lie behind them. He fails to

act on his resolve to 'sweep to my revenge'. He tests the King's guilt by a means which reveals that Hamlet knows his secret, and convinces him that Hamlet must be destroyed. Sparing him in the prayer scene, Hamlet leaves him alive to plot and eventually achieve that destruction. He provides him with the accomplice he needs: killing Polonius, and by that and his cruel behaviour driving Ophelia mad, he raises up Laertes as their avenger and an instrument for the king. Finally, he fails to obey his premonition about the fencing match, and to 'peruse the foils'.

These errors cannot be referred to one sole 'flaw' in Hamlet. Some do him honour; none, in origin, is wholly to his discredit. Making use of the players shows the same power of seizing an opportunity as, later, making use of the pirates. He is rightly conscientious in requiring confirmation of Claudius's guilt. It is a tragic fact, and *Hamlet* illustrates it, that what is noblest in a man may contribute to undo him. His mother's conduct upon his father's death, and the Ghost's revelation of her adultery, sickens him with marriage, sex, and procreation. Projecting Gertrude's sex-guilt upon women in general, and upon Ophelia as a future Gertrude, he savages the appeal ('Here's metal more attractive') that she still has for him. The revelation of his adored father's murder generates for the murderer a fanatical hatred that finds vent in his motive for sparing him, and for not pausing to make sure of the eavesdropper's identity.

Consider Hamlet's self-accusations. Some you dismiss: he is not a coward, does not – as you have just seen – 'lack gall'! But when Hamlet speaks of 'thinking too precisely on th'event' the play confirms him: to act with decision he has had to act on the spur of the moment, killing Polonius, boarding the pirate, killing the King. The charge of procrastination he repeats against himself is confirmed by the Ghost who reproaches him with his 'almost blunted purpose'. In the normal Hamlet portrayed by Ophelia (III.i.152–6) there was nothing to unfit him for the situation he has to meet. It is part of his tragedy that the very disclosure of the situation and the duty consequently laid upon him are what disable him.

Without the nobility, genius, and attractiveness of Hamlet you would not feel either the tragic waste of his catastrophe or tragic exaltation in the value of his life which survives his tragic death. Besides, Denmark is cleansed; a fresh start will be made under a monarch far different from Claudius. Hamlet has accomplished his task. He died reconciled with Laertes, and to the human condition of mingled sin and virtue; and accepting the co-operation of Providence with human purpose. His worth, already honoured by Fortinbras, will have public tribute from him, and from Horatio who best knows it. So, fittingly, ends a tragedy and tragic hero.

5.3 THE PLACE OF COMEDY IN THE TRAGEDY

Hamlet is one of three Shakespearean tragedies in which the comic is brought into the heart of the tragedy. There are two Clown parts. One is countrified and earthy, the other a fantastical courtier. The Gravedigger stands in the grave he has dug for the heroine, and has a comic discussion of her drowning (in which he is wrong about it). Osric brings the hero the proposition which will be his death, and leaves with his acceptance of it. The scene of the catastrophe follows. The turning-point of the tragedy has been the death of the frequently-comic Polonius at the hands of the hero. Hamlet cries, as he finishes off the royal murderer, 'Is thy union here?' Though Elizabethan puns were not necessarily funny, the wit here is barbed with a touch of sardonic comedy, furiously savage as it is. Hamlet the tragic protagonist is responsible for much of the humour. He plays the comedian in his 'antic disposition' and in baiting Osric, Rosencrantz and Guildenstern, Polonius, and the King.

The comedy is of various kinds. Some of these may be illustrated:

Comedy of language, as in Osric's 'Three of the carriages are very dear to fancy'; the phrase, Hamlet objects, would be apt 'if we could carry cannon by our sides'.

The comedy of cross-questions and crooked answers, played in more than one encounter between Hamlet and the King.

Comic stage business, like Hamlet's with the recorder: 'Look you, these are the stops'. He pretends he is seeking to overcome Guildenstern's false modesty; and Guildenstern's incapacity, when confronted with the 'prop', has some affinity with the routine of the clown baffled by an implement he cannot master.

Comedy of character: Osric and the Gravedigger are comic 'character parts'. Finer comedy, because more complex, is the character of Polonius. In family affairs his counsel is not unsound in its worldly way, but is stereotyped. He is comically self-satisfied and garrulous – a wiseacre.

Comedy of situation: Recognising 'how pregnant sometimes' Hamlet's replies are, Polonius thinks them the random hits of madness, whereas they are pertinently directed by a Hamlet who (allowing for his obsession with sexual corruption) is sane enough.

Appearance and reality: a comic as well as a tragic theme. Polonius there mistook for reality an appearance of madness. Even Hamlet's tragic error of mistaken identity in killing Polonius has its ironically comic aspect, voiced in 'rash intruding fool' and 'I'll lug the guts into the neighbour room' where he will be 'At supper . . . Not where he eats, but where a is eaten'.

All this comedy in a tragedy is not mere 'comic relief'. It does bring an element of relief, but it may better be called 'comic counterpoise': a counterweight which keeps poised at its proper height the tragedy of the play. As the catastrophe approaches, it is the kind of 'levity by which the seriousness', says T. S. Eliot, 'is intensified'.

6 RESPONSES TO *HAMLET*

6.1 PROBLEMS AND NON-PROBLEMS

For the student, *Hamlet* presents problems of interpretation which arise, some of them inescapably from the text, some from critical commentary or the acting tradition. This second kind divide into those worth taking seriously, and those which have to be discussed solely in order to dismiss them. Non-problems have their origin sometimes in doubts or questions the play does not admit.

It does invite questions which are worth raising because the attempt to answer them leads straight into the heart of the drama. Why does Hamlet delay? Why is he so cruel to Ophelia? Whether Hamlet is really mad, a question still occasionally heard, cannot survive either the objection that to be dramatic the hero must be responsible for his actions, or the evidence of the play. Gertrude is warned not to lay 'that flattering unction' to her soul, and what Hamlet was overheard speaking was not, says Claudius, 'like madness'. But re-formulated, as whether the 'antic disposition' is always wholly assumed, the question has point. In it he can discharge the heightened tension you see on his return from the Ghost, and after the success of the play scene - perhaps in the whole sequence where revenge-passion possesses him in sparing the King and killing Polonius. He is on edge, comes at times to the brink, but never actually goes over.

Hamlet's age, belatedly put at thirty by the Gravedigger's reminiscences, which contradict the many implications of a youthful Hamlet, is a problem for the modern actor, who must look one age or the other. It was none for the audience who saw Burbage, and placed his Hamlet within the range his appearance indicated. The dramatic point of the reference is not, as critics have thought, deliberately to fix Hamlet's age, but to juxtapose King Hamlet's victory, Hamlet's birth, and the date when the Gravedigger began digging graves. A striking discrepancy is between the Horatio who is familiar with the Danish situation and the Horatio who is not, according to the play's need of him at the time: the one to enlighten Marcellus and

Barnardo, the other to be a recipient of Hamlet's exposition. Is there discrepancy between the hotheaded Fortinbras, sharker-up of 'lawless resolutes', and the subsequent King-apparent, general of a disciplined army? The contrast may mean that Shakespeare changed his mind. If so, did Shakespeare not bother to conform the earlier Fortinbras to the later; or is there no discrepancy, Shakespeare having intended the development from the start?

Two problems which, again not unreasonably, have troubled directors, are why Claudius betrays no reaction to the dumb-show, and on what does Hamlet focus Gertrude's attention with 'Look here upon this picture, and on this'. Desperate remedies have been adopted for the first: preoccupied with Gertrude, Claudius does not attend to the dumb-show; or even does not see it, sight-lines not permitting. Neither is credible of a state occasion as an Elizabethan dramatist would understand it. A psychological explanation is persuasive. Claudius has the strongest motive for believing as long as he can that the performance mirrors his crime only by coincidence; and when it begins to perturb him, for controlling his perturbation. Jenkins, however, rejects this explanation as intruding real life into a situation the play deliberately ignores. 'This picture' and 'this' were presented by John Gielgud to the mind's eye only; Derek Jacobi, following one stage tradition, had them as paintings on the wall. Another, making them miniatures, seems preferable. The words suggest stage business with hand-properties for focus; miniatures, of which the audience can see nothing, cannot compete with the images Hamlet's descriptions create.

It is even more essential that the audience should see the Ghost. Nervous of their disbelief in the supernatural, modern directors have sometimes made it an invisible projection of Hamlet's mind, disregarding a text in which it is seen by a group and impersonated by an actor. This not only throws Shakespeare to the winds; it will not work in the closet scene, where a visible Ghost seen by Hamlet is required to make the dramatic point that Gertrude cannot see it. The non-problem of which among Elizabethan beliefs it conforms to (Catholic, Protestant, or other) is touched on briefly in the Commentary, and discussed – as a problem – in Dover Wilson's *What Happens in Hamlet*, ch. III.

Other questions which have no existence for the dramatist arise only when the play is taken out of the theatre where it belongs, and scrutinised in the study as though it ought to meet requirements which apply to documentaries recording actual life, or to the many novels and limited number of plays that aim at a naturalistic illusion of it. Only an eyewitness could have furnished Gertrude's report of Ophelia's death: why did he make no attempt to save her? But what fills the audience's minds is the pathos and poetry of the scene; they are not wondering how Gertrude came by her knowledge of it. To complain of the utter improbability of Laertes and Hamlet having heard nothing of Ophelia's madness is misplaced naturalism. That they should be taken by surprise is what dramatic impact demands.

Of what ought now to be recognised as non-problems in *Hamlet*, the most famous is that of Hamlet and the eavesdroppers. To some, both in the theatre and the study, it seems that Hamlet changed his tone to Ophelia after his question 'Where's your father?' and her false reply, and that his abrupt question itself was unaccounted for unless at that point Polonius betrayed himself: to have him do so became a stage tradition. Dover Wilson, perceiving that Hamlet's later tone to Ophelia is only a development of his earlier one, concluded that he must have known her a decoy from the first, and made him overhear the eavesdropping plan when it was concocted, 570 lines before. To both suppositions there is a fatal objection. It was a convention of Elizabethan drama, demonstrated by Dame Helen Gardner ('Lawful Espials', *Modern Language Review*, XXXIII, 1938) that in eavesdropping scenes, who is aware of whom is made known to the audience: in this scene, they are reminded that the espials will be overhearing Hamlet, but nowhere informed that he is or becomes aware of them. Further, while Dover Wilson was right to see no discontinuity in Hamlet's attitude to Ophelia, Hamlet's suspicion of her is not as a decoy: it is of her sexual nature. Sharing his mother's she will, unless she takes refuge in a nunnery, come to share her sexual delinquency. 'Are you honest?', half a dozen speeches before the question about her father, springs clearly from that obsessive belief, and so does what he says afterwards; which at 'I have heard of your paintings' has him no longer seeing her as an indidivual, but abusing in her the whole guilty sex he has identified with his mother. But does not the abruptness of 'Where's your father?' require a glimpse of him as cue? Hamlet's question depends on no outside stimulus; it comes from within a mind liable at any moment to fly from daughter to father as abruptly as at II.ii.182, 'Have you a daughter?' and (400) 'O Jephthah . . . what a treasure hadst thou' it flies from father to daughter, both times with reference to virginity. Distinct from Hamlet's impulse to ask the question, Shakespeare's purpose in it is to remind the *audience* where Polonius is. It is they who, in order to savour the ironies, need to be aware of it, not Hamlet; were he aware, the ironies would be blunted.

6.2 CRITICAL APPRAISALS

During the eighteenth century many of the long-lived problems and non-problems concerning Hamlet were raised: his delay, irresolution, alleged inconsistency of character. His appalling reason for sparing the King at prayer is already explained away. He is romantically unfitted for his situation by the refinement of his moral nature, as for Coleridge (1818, 1827) by his sensibility, introversion, and because 'every incident sets him thinking'. It is not only for his task that the Hamlet of the Romantic critics is unfit. The stage, according to Charles Lamb (1811) cannot present him without loss of everything that makes Shakespeare's creation exceptional: what, he asks, have the physical gifts of the actor 'to do with Hamlet? . . . to do with intellect?'

This divorce from the stage was authoritatively reversed by Granville Barker (1930). Meanwhile Bradley (1904) had made clear how much the romantic and sentimental conception of Hamlet's character ignored: his 'embitterment', the 'callousness, grossness, brutality' he sometimes shows; his lightning actions of stabbing the eavesdropper, boarding the pirate; the man before whom, as he kills Claudius, 'all the court stands helpless' and who 'in the throes of death has force and fire enough to wrest the cup from Horatio's hand'.

Nineteenth-century critics identified fresh problems. Was Hamlet's madness wholly feigned? Did he become aware of the eavesdroppers in the nunnery scene? Not all were about Hamlet – why did Claudius not react to the dumb-show? But the play *Hamlet* came to be first and foremost Prince Hamlet. With Coleridge and the Germans leading the way, two interests chiefly engaged the critics. Pursuing Hamlet's thoughts on the enigma of life, they philosophised; but above all they diagnosed his character.

The best guide through the most significant twentieth-century *Hamlet* criticism up to the mid 1960s, as indeed to the whole tradition since Shakespeare's time, is Harold Jenkins's essay 'Hamlet Then till Now' in *Shakespeare Survey*, 18 (1965). In reaction against the obsession with the famous 'truth-to-life' of Shakespeare's characters it was insisted that prior to being lifelike they were working parts of a play, to be understood in terms of their functions in its dramatic action and pattern. Another reaction was against a Hamlet (mainly in performance) who never alienated sympathy. Both Prince and play were put in their Elizabethan context; Elizabethan melancholy and Elizabethan ghosts were comprehensively studied, with results now fruitful, now misapplied. Caroline Spurgeon (1930, 1935) and W. H. Clemen (1936, 1951) developed to great purpose the investigation of Shakespeare's imagery and its integration with his dramatic purposes. The 'principle of analogy' in Shakespeare, remarked on by Hazlitt (1817), received its due when G. Wilson Knight and Una Ellis-Fermor laid stress on what they called his 'spatial' structure. The most striking advance in the interpretation of *Hamlet* is made in Jenkins's critical introduction to his edition (1982), where he shows the central significance of the dual role of Hamlet as revenger and object of revenge – a man whose duty is also a crime to be paid for with his life.

6.3 *HAMLET* IN THE THEATRE

In the theatre *Hamlet* has had an unbroken and illuminating history. In the seventeenth century it was on the stage that it made its greatest impact. Betterton, the next great Hamlet after Burbage for whom the part was written, no doubt inherited a tradition from the original performances. From Betterton onward, every leading actor sought to excel as Hamlet, and except for Kemble, Edmund Kean, and Macready, they did. Impressions of how some of them played the part, or some episodes in it, have reached us from eyewitnesses: for Betterton, Colley Cibber; for Garrick, G. T. Lichtenberg and Arthur Murphy; for Henry Irving, his Ophelia, Ellen Terry; for Tomaso Salvini, G. H. Lewes; and for Barry Sullivan, Irving and Salvini, George Bernard Shaw. Each of these Hamlets was a riveting physical exhibition of the actor's art. Forbes-Robertson's innovatory Hamlet of 1897 proved him, wrote Shaw, a classical actor: one who 'can present a dramatic hero . . . whose passions are those which have produced the philosophy, the poetry, the art and statecraft of the world, and not merely . . . its weddings, coroner's inquests and executions'. Betterton's performance was notable for its 'mien of majesty'; his voice was 'of more strength than melody', but its controlled tempo could lead up to 'an artful climax which enforced universal attention'. 'When Garrick entered the scene, the character he assumed was legible in his countenance'; 'he never drops his character when he has finished a speech', but, like Burbage before him, remained 'the very man'. Kean's Hamlet was but a sequence of impressive moments; Kemble presented only the introspective and melancholy aspects; Macready's was 'lachrymose and fretful'. The art of Salvini's performance, says Shaw, 'was beyond all praise'; but Lewes and he agree that it did not create a Hamlet resembling Shakespeare's: 'the many-sidedness' writes Lewes, 'was sadly truncated'. Irving obliterated Shakespeare's character by his own conception – that of Hamlet always the lover.

From Betterton to Irving and later, the actors had not been appearing in *Hamlet* as Shakespeare designed it, but in adaptations matched to the taste of the time, or when in the course of the nineteenth century these were discarded, in versions drastically cut to allow of setting elaborate spectacular and realistic scenes in the prolonged intervals. In 1881, with William Poel's *Hamlet* from the First Quarto (now known to be, though an actor's version, an unauthorised and garbled one) a momentous revolution began, in a very small way. What he and his Elizabethan Stage Society of amateurs did to start the recovery of a true Shakespeare lay partly in a respect for the full text, partly in 'the new rapid delivery of the verse', but above all, as J. L. Styan insists, 'in the permanent stage set which revealed . . . the structure of the play' by making it possible to recover 'the original rhythmic continuity of scene upon scene'. Granville Barker developed these reforms and succeeded eventually in carrying them into the professional theatre. Nowadays in Shakespeare we expect the continuous playing on which Shakespeare reckoned: we do not expect scenic illusion. Poel's actors wore Elizabethan dress, Shakespeare's a sometimes modified and, where appropriate, a rich version of it. In 1925 the Birmingham Repertory Theatre staged *Hamlet* in modern dress, and the experiment has been followed; but though the Elizabethan costume of Shakespeare's actors was modern to his audience, they expected it: any value in a modern-dress *Hamlet* today lies in shaking the audience out of its expectations.

Within the past half-century, Hamlet has been played by three Shake-speareans no less great than any of their predecessors. But though in a succession of Shakespearean tragic roles Sir Laurence Olivier has touched the heights, his film Hamlet (1948) was not among them. Too much was excluded by a characterisation narrowly keyed to the concept of 'a man who could not make up his mind'. Sir Michael Redgrave's stage Hamlet of 1950 was finely judged. At his entry, grief paralysing his will was plain to see. His heartbroken love cried out 'father!' to an unresponsive Ghost. In the closet scene, it was an angry tenderness, untainted by Freudian lust, that spoke in his reproof to his mother. This Hamlet grew, from his appalled inaction, to the self-mastery of the last Act. He was no weakling, but a tragic hero; not however romantically simplified like the Edwardian Hamlets against whom Gielgud reacted from the time, a young man of twenty-five (the Edwardians were forty and upward), he first played the part in 1929. In productions then and in 1934–7, 1939, and 1944 Sir John established himself as the foremost Hamlet of his day. For his performances of 1934–7, Rosamond Gilder has furnished a scene-by-scene appreciation, supplemented by comments of his own on costume, scenery, and stage business. Like Redgrave, he is a classical actor in the same sense as Forbes Robertson. His Hamlets have realised, in convincing stage terms, a unified conception of the character, the most comprehensive ever achieved, unless (which we have no means of knowing) by Burbage with Shakespeare to direct him. He deliberately restored to the part, as he says, 'the unpleasant aspects of Hamlet's character; . . . the violent and ugly colours' without, of course, allowing them to dominate the rest.

That was the distortion in Derek Jacobi's talented 1977 performance. His Prince, said the Guardian critic, was an 'emotionally retarded' person-ality, whose grief and rage in the nunnery scene were of a childish sort, whose closet scene was Freudianly incestuous, and beneath whose pretence of madness real madness never ceased to lurk. Other recent Hamlets have suffered from the permissiveness which has become the chief enemy, on stage, of Shakespeare's dramatic art. When Dover Wilson writes, 'Of a role so indeterminate almost any version is possible', H. D. F. Kitto retorts 'Perhaps any version can be made effective on the stage – but only to an audience which does not very much mind whether the play as a whole makes sense or not'. Of David Warner's Hamlet in Peter Hall's 1965 production The Times critic wrote, 'it makes sense, and it connects with a widespread attitude to political life. And yet how much the play has had to be tailored to fit the interpretation'. With Roger Rees, Michael Billington observes (Guardian, 18 April 1985) 'we seem to have passed through' the Nicol Williamson and Jonathan Pryce 'age of the angry young Hamlets . . . He gives Hamlet a noble heart'. Yet de Jongh's interview (Guardian, 24 August 1984) shows Rees and Ron Daniels the director preoccupied with their disappointment (and perhaps their generation's) of the hopes they worked for at the end of the sixties: they have felt fully entitled, it appears, to seize on Hamlet as a channel for that preoccupation, without regard for what Shakespeare may be saying through this play. Yet as a student of *Hamlet* it will pay you to take any opportunities you have of seeing it acted. If a production is good, and Shakespearean, it will teach you a great deal you can learn in no other way; if it is not, you will learn from asking yourself where it is wrong and why. For your business is to understand *Shakespeare's* dramatic art.

Theatre criticism

> [Richard Burbage is] gone and with him
> . . . young Hamlett . . ..
> Oft have I seene him leap into the grave,
> Suiting the person which he seem'd to have
> Of a sadd lover with soe true an eye,
> That theer I would have sworne he meant to dye.
>
> (John Fletcher? c.1619)

[Garrick, seeing the Ghost, gives a supreme exhibition of terror and astonishment.] At length he speaks, not at the beginning but at the end of a breath, with a trembling voice, 'Angels and ministers of grace, defend us'.

(Georg C. Lichtenberg, 1775)

The character of Polonius . . . actors have often misrepresented. Shakespeare never intended to represent him as a buffoon.

(S. T. Coleridge, 1813)

Nothing is more peculiarly individual to . . . Hamlet than the manner in which he at times shuts up with a snap . . . the poetic or philosophic stop, and pulls out the fantastic or cynical. This side of a many-sided mind . . . Mr. Irving has distinctly worked up . . . since his earlier performances.

(*Vanity Fair*, 11 Jan. 1879)

I gave Forbes [Robertson] a description of what the end should be like. Fortinbras with a winged helmet and Hamlet carried off on the shields, with 'the ordnance shot off within' just as the wily William planned it . . . My idea seems to have come off.

(George Bernard Shaw, 1897)

The players . . . form a stock commedia dell'arte company. 'He that plays the King', 'the adventurous knight', the sighing lover, the humorous man i.e. the elderly pantaloon, the clown, and the lady.

(J. Isaacs, 1927)

Realistic likelihood will always give way to dramatic effect.

(H. Granville Barker, 1930)

There is such a range of opportunity in the part that it encourages you to try all sorts of different tricks and effects.

(Sir John Gielgud, 1979)

Stripped and pummelled cruelly by [Claudius] after Polonius's murder, [Alan Howard's Hamlet] is tamed, stunned into conformity. A white, brainwashed figure, . . . he will play this society's game with it: deceive, smile, kill.

(Ronald Bryden, *Observer*, 7 June 1970)

Albert Finney's performance restores . . . [to] the play, a sense of danger . . . He makes you believe that the killer instinct is doing genuine battle with sovereign reason.

(Michael Billington, *Guardian*, reviewing the National Theatre production of 1975/6)

The Hamlet of Roger Rees . . . is a fevered genius of a portrayal . . . His conveyance of preoccupation and his sudden outcrops of raw passion are really mesmeric.

(J. F. Turner, *Plays and Players*, June 1985)

6.4   THREE ACTORS ON PLAYING HAMLET

The complexity of Hamlet's character presents a great challenge to actors. Consider the validity of the following interpretations given by three Hamlets of the last ten years, interviewed by the author in 1983/4. Points taken from the interviews are necessarily selective.

Martin Jarvis

Martin Jarvis played Hamlet as 'a young man of strength and power; honest and direct, and not mad'. An exploration of the *brink* between madness and sanity made sense to him. A tight control of strain marked the nunnery scene, even though the actor's assumption that Hamlet knew he was being spied on led to physical violence towards Ophelia. To this Hamlet, his meeting with the Ghost first exposed the 'edge of mental control' in danger. His heightened excitement gives birth to the idea of the 'antic disposition' to cover his purpose, but his feigned madness is never confused with 'brink' situations. Having established his antic disposition, Hamlet 'becomes, in a sense, imprisoned in his role. It is obvious to the audience what he is doing with Rosencrantz and Guildenstern, but to outsiders, he is talking in riddles'. His riddling farewell to Claudius as 'dear mother' (IV.iii.52) was marked by this Hamlet with a long, deliberate kiss, which said plainly 'If kisses could kill. . .!' Martin Jarvis sees 'To be or not to be' as a deliberation about killing or not killing Claudius: his Hamlet is not suicidal. He tried to give some sense of Hamlet's normal potential, 'because you never see Hamlet at his best in the play; you see a sullied man on a downward spiral'.

Jack Shepherd
Jack Shepherd, very aware of Hamlet's bewildering variety – 'you know Shakespeare's going to treat you like a punch-bag, send you in all different directions' – found 'a psychological framework to work on' in Hamlet's maturing process – 'it's a play about growing up', and 'a streak of genuine madness' pushing Hamlet over the brink. He is 'obviously feigning with Rosencrantz and Guildenstern but surely he's mad when he makes morbid jokes about worms to Claudius' and in the nunnery scene he's 'objectively crazy'. He 'thinks he's getting rid of Ophelia for her own good'. But Hamlet is really rejecting Ophelia because 'she's become a nuisance and he can't cope with a woman of his own age'. He successfully copes with his mother in the closet scene: there the basis of his attack is 'jealousy – "Why have you chosen another man instead of me?" ' Jack Shepherd sees Hamlet's tragedy in that he was 'killed at the moment when he's got rid of all his problems: he would have made a truly great king'.

Derek Jacobi
The most unusual feature of Derek Jacobi's Hamlet was that he spoke the soliloquy 'To be or not to be' to Ophelia. This staging helped him engender the complex passion necessary to 'launch into the huge horror to come in the rest of the scene'. He believes that Hamlet and Ophelia have been lovers in the fullest sense. 'This is perhaps his last chance to say to someone who loved him, "Look, this is what's wrong with me. I'm contemplating suicide. Just listen!" At the end of his huge journey through the speech, she's just heard the man she loves say "I'd like to commit suicide", what does she say? – "How have you been keeping lately?" – "I've just been telling you!" He doesn't need to see the arras twitch to know something's very wrong'.

7 SPECIMEN PASSAGE AND COMMENTARY

The example below shows the kind of close critical attention needed to analyse the text. During the course of your study the *entire* text should have been subjected to close scrutiny, with the aid of a good annotated edition and a reputable dictionary (for example, the *Oxford English Dictionary* in several volumes) which will help you with unfamiliar sentence constructions and obscure words. Pay particular attention to words you *think* you understand, but which have changed their meaning since Shakespeare's day. 'Th'extravagant and erring spirit' (I.i.159) does *not* infer that the Ghost overspent his allowance on sinful pursuits!

On a passage set for comment, the answer should be as organised as the answer to an essay question. A running commentary – a series of remarks on features as you come to them – is not good enough. You will notice them in that order as you read the passage through: that is the *first* stage. Then your comments will need grouping under topics, and for the topics you will have to decide an order for which the examiner can see reason. It will help you if you approach the passage with a plan of things to look for and to do. If the question gives specific instructions, follow them in what you include, and arrange your answer to meet them. Unless they direct you otherwise, you will probably be expected:

(i) to place the passage in its *immediate* context. Be brief. Do not go back beyond what has just been happening to account for who is on stage, what the situation is, and how it governs their speeches and anything they do;

(ii) to indicate what the passage contributes to the play as a whole. If it marks a stage or turning-point in the play's progress, say how. Ask yourself what it does to build on and develop what has gone before, and prepare for what is to come. See whether anything in it forms part of the symmetric structure of correspondences, or dramatises a principal theme;

(iii) to consider, in order to comment on the substance of the passage, whether it helps to characterise the speakers; in what ways it is

     designed to appeal to the audience; and if the dramatist is making
     use in it of the resources of his theatre;

(iv) to examine the style: the way language, sentence structure, rhythmic
     stress, changes from prose to verse, and the like, create dramatic
     effects such as mood, tension, irony, climax.

On (ii), (iii), (iv) you will find detailed guidance in 4, *Technical features*.

Warning 1: Do not allow a planned approach such as this to make you
force upon the passage something it does not contain, nor blind you to
something in it the plan does not cover.

Warning 2: - an elementary one: *do not paraphrase* (that is, merely put
into other words what the passage says). Your answer is not to translate it,
but to present the results of studying it.

Specimen passage

HAMLET   Thus conscience does make cowards of us all,
        And thus the native hue of resolution
        Is sicklied o'er with the pale cast of thought,   85
        And enterprises of great pitch and moment
        With this regard their currents turn awry
        And lose the name of action. Soft you now,
        The fair Ophelia! Nymph, in thy orisons
        Be all my sins remembered.
OPHELIA   Good my lord,   90
        How does your honour for this many a day?
HAMLET   I humbly thank you, well.
OPHELIA   My lord, I have remembrances of yours
        That I have longed long to redeliver.
        I pray you now receive them.
HAMLET   No, not I.   95
        I never gave you aught.
OPHELIA   My honour'd lord, you know right well you did,
        And with them words of so sweet breath compos'd
        As made the things more rich. Their perfume lost,
        Take these again; for to the noble mind   100
        Rich gifts wax poor when givers prove unkind.
        There, my lord.
HAMLET   Ha, ha! Are you honest?
OPHELIA   My lord?
HAMLET   Are you fair?   105
OPHELIA   What means your lordship?
HAMLET   That if you be honest and fair, your honesty should admit
        no discourse to your beauty.
OPHELIA   Could beauty, my lord, have better commerce than with
        honesty?   110

HAMLET   Ay, truly, for the power of beauty will sooner transform
honesty from what it is to a bawd than the force of honesty can
translate beauty into his likeness. This was sometime a paradox,
but now the time gives it proof. I did love you once.
OPHELIA   Indeed, my lord, you made me believe so.
HAMLET   You should not have believed me; for virtue cannot so
inoculate our old stock but we shall relish of it. I loved you not.
OPHELIA   I was the more deceived.   120
HAMLET   Get thee to a nunnery. Why, wouldst thou be a breeder of
sinners? I am myself indifferent honest, but yet I could accuse me
of such things that it were better my mother had not borne me.

(III.i.83–124)

Commentary

In fulfilment of Polonius's plan, accepted by Claudius to test his conviction that Hamlet is mad for love of Ophelia, she is walking, as directed,
intent apparently upon a book of devotion, where Hamlet will encounter
her. The two 'lawful espials' have concealed themselves, so as to observe
his behaviour to her. Hamlet has entered, not noticing Ophelia who is well
upstage, and soliloquises: 'To be, or not to be'. The argument he has been
having with himself is not about a decision of his own: it is on why men,
with so many motives for death, and the means easy to come by, acquiesce
in continuing to live (as, for all his death-wish, he himself does).

'Thus' indicates that the given passage begins with his summing up.
Conscience makes cowards 'of us all', he generalises: because we fear, not
death in itself, but what conscience tells us about death – that it may not
be the end – and what our deserts may be in afterlife. As conscience
inhibits the action of taking one's life, so other crucial actions are inhibited
by reflection (85–8). The soliloquy and its summing up are not intended
to advance the plot, but to place in the most universal of contexts, at this
central point of the drama, the profoundest issue for Hamlet and the play:
whether man's plight is better escaped from or endured. Picturing solely
the ills of life, it develops the sickened vision that has been his since his
opening scene, and though in giving its verdict for acceptance (as the lesser
evil) it points distantly forward to his far different acceptance in Act V, it
prepares for that sickened vision to dominate his encounter with Ophelia.
That encounter does advance both plots, which it unites: the revenge plot,
and the love-relationship with which the part here given is mainly concerned, leading on to what Hamlet says further on: the married 'all but
one shall live', which assures Claudius of the threat he presents.

'Soft you now,/The fair Ophelia' signals the beginning of the dialogue
for which you have been kept waiting. By the first sentences, Shakespeare
defines the preoccupations of each speaker: Hamlet's sense of 'sins', of
contamination; Ophelia's wounded love, hinted in the 'many a day' she has
known nothing of him. Three phases of dialogue follow. First comes the
ritual return of gifts: Hamlet's initial refusal makes them visible images of

his rejection, and her wounded love becomes explicit. More generalised debate on 'honesty' (chastity) and 'beauty' follows, Hamlet allowing his jaundiced belief in the destiny of all fair women to permit no escape for Ophelia from it except to a nunnery. This, in the third movement of the encounter, again directly personal, makes his rejection decisive. Ophelia's reticent pain, recalling his courtship, is part of the tragic march of cause and effect: it is one of the causes of her madness, which in turn reinforces Laertes' purpose of revenge.

Hamlet's attack on Ophelia, with his feeling about Gertrude at the back of it, is matched in the closet scene by his attack on Gertrude herself. The two matched episodes belong to the play's symmetric structure. The present eavesdropping scene, with Polonius an 'espial', looks back to his setting a spy on Laertes, and forward to his fatal eavesdropping in Gertrude's closet. Many of the correspondences are similarly preparatory. Hamlet's cruelty to Ophelia, insisting that her natural destiny is to lose her virtue, worsens in the play scene, where he treats her as though she had already lost it. His contradictions, 'I did love you once', 'I loved you not', will be repudiated over her corpse. The urging to a nunnery is prophetic. Ophelia is indeed buried as a virgin, not figuratively in a convent, but literally in her grave. Two of the images in the given passage belong to series that run throughout the play: 'sicklied o'er' to the imagery of disease; the 'old' 'infected stock' to the imagery of evil in garden and orchard. The 'currents' turned 'awry' have a counterpart in the sea-image for Laertes' current turned 'awry' not into inaction but into rebellion: the ocean 'eats not the flats with more impetuous haste'.

Ophelia is here characterised as possessing a quiet strength she has often been thought to lack. She will not take Hamlet's repulse of the gifts, but persists: 'There, my lord'. Nor will she let him maintain he has no memory of courting her: 'you know right well you did', When he begins his argument on 'honesty' and 'beauty' her re-statement of how the two are related contrasts the normality of her view with the perversity of his. The conclusion of his soliloquy shows his breadth of mind, transcending merely personal concerns to take up an issue and debate it in universal terms; and his power finally to draw a conclusion – 'Thus'. But otherwise, the aspects of his character which those final lines bring to mind are scarcely favourable. The death-wish is rejected, but only from 'cowardice' (not common-or-garden cowardice, however). 'Enterprises' losing 'the name of action' recall his procrastination; and the reason, what he is to call his 'thinking too precisely on th'event'. In the dialogue, he begins with his 'sins' and recurs to them; he is given, notably in the third and seventh soliloquies, to self-accusation. And throughout, he cannot digest his sense of contamination. His generalising habit of mind, a merit in the soliloquy, here has been disastrous.

The sense of contamination, and the share of sin in the human condition, is a theme central to the play which the given passage brings out. Another is the blunting of resolution, commented upon in the last lines of the soliloquy, and the frustration of purpose, seen in the abortion of Hamlet's and Ophelia's love. Hamlet believes the appearance of a private interview is a reality; she and the audience know it is not. His response to her 'orisons' is a sympathetic touch; but they too are an appearance.

Her book of devotion, a stage property, in its use as a cue for comment, is an example of Shakespeare's stagecraft. The mere appearance of devoutness it gives her, suggesting orisons, is the cue for Hamlet to speak of 'my sins'. Ophelia's other 'prop', the gifts, when he rejects their return, furnish a visual image of *his* rejection of *her*. He must take them at 'There, my lord'; if not, there seems no satisfactory way of getting them off-stage; but the point has been made. The stagecraft of the scene depends on two Elizabethan stage conventions. One determines that Hamlet is not aware of eavesdroppers: in Elizabethan eavesdropping scenes, who is aware of whom is always made plain to the audience. The other is soliloquy itself. Though this one is not spoken 'at' the audience, Hamlet, at the front of the stage at the mid-point among them, is not simply being overheard by them; he is communicating with them in a special relationship.

The soliloquy is in eloquent blank verse: Ophelia's maxim in a rhyming couplet concludes the aptly constrained verse with which the dialogue begins. The change to prose seems to come when a fresh affectation of 'antic disposition' combines with what is really disturbing Hamlet's mind to make the orderliness of verse inappropriate. The prose has its patterns no less than the poetry created largely by repetition of key words, with shifting meanings for 'honest', 'honesty', 'discourse', 'commerce', and what Hamlet confesses to be 'a paradox'. He employs equivocations. 'I never gave you aught' is factually untrue. 'I loved you not' must have equivocal meaning, since he has already admitted that in the ordinary sense 'I did love you once'. From images already commented upon, both prose and poetry gain vividness: one of them, 'honesty' translated to 'a bawd' is a personification.

REVISION QUESTIONS

1. What characteristics of *Hamlet* make Hamlet so central to the play?

2.   'Lay not that flattering unction to your soul
That not your trespass but my madness speaks' (Hamlet)
'This mad young man' (Claudius)

   What view does the play persuade you to take of Hamlet's 'antic disposition'?

3. What is the dramatic significance of Polonius and his family in *Hamlet*?

4. 'It would be wrong to think of Claudius merely as a conventional villain. In spite of his sin, he shows some of the qualities of a good king, and is to be pitied for his personal tragedy of a guilty conscience'. How far do you agree with this view?

5. 'Three young men in search of revenge'. How adequate is this view of *Hamlet*?

6. 'There is no mystery in *Hamlet*: it is the story of a courageous prince who finds it understandably hard to take revenge on a shrewd and powerful king.' How adequate is this description of the play?

7. Do you agree that 'after the death of Polonius the action of *Hamlet* tends to disintegrate'?

8. 'The action and dialogue of *Hamlet* express the cruel, frustrating experience of living: the soliloquies merely reinforce the impression'. Do you agree with this view of their relationship?

9. 'In *Hamlet* no action produces the result its perpetrator intends and all actions seem inevitably to lead to the final tragedy' Discuss.

10. 'Elsinore is full of actors.' Assess the dramatic and thematic importance to *Hamlet* of (i) the Players and their plays, and (ii) the 'acting' of one other character.

11. Consider some of the ways in which Shakespeare makes dramatic the theme of the relationship between appearance and reality in *Hamlet*.

12. Consider some of the dramatic uses of verse and prose in *Hamlet*.

APPENDIX:

SHAKESPEARE'S THEATRE

We should speak, as Muriel Bradbrook reminds us, not of the Elizabethan stage but of Elizabethan stages. Plays of Shakespeare were acted on tour, in the halls of mansions, one at least in Gray's Inn, frequently at Court, and after 1609 at the Blackfriars, a small, roofed theatre for those who could afford the price. But even after his Company acquired the Blackfriars, we know of no play of his not acted (unless, rather improbably, *Troilus* is an exception) for the general public at the Globe, or before 1599 at its predecessor, The Theatre, which, since the Globe was constructed from the same timbers, must have resembled it. Describing the Globe, we can claim therefore to be describing, in an acceptable sense, Shakespeare's theatre, the physical structure his plays were designed to fit. Even in the few probably written for a first performance elsewhere, adaptability to that structure would be in his mind.

For the facilities of the Globe we have evidence from the drawing of the Swan theatre (based on a sketch made by a visitor to London about 1596) which depicts the interior of another public theatre; the builder's contract for the Fortune theatre, which in certain respects (fortunately including the dimensions and position of the stage) was to copy the Globe; indications in the dramatic texts; comments, like Ben Jonson's on the throne let down from above by machinery; and eye-witness testimony to the number of spectators (in round figures, 3000) accommodated in the auditorium.

In communicating with the audience, the actor was most favourably placed. Soliloquising at the centre of the front of the great platform, he was at the mid-point of the theatre, with no one among the spectators more than sixty feet away from him. That platform-stage (Figs I and II) was the most important feature for performance at the Globe. It had the audience – standing in the yard (10) and seated in the galleries (9) – on three sides of it. It was 43 feet wide, and 27½ feet from front to back. Raised (?5½ feet) above the level of the yard, it had a trap-door (II.8) giving access to the space below it. The actors, with their equipment, occupied the 'tiring house' (attiring-house: 2) immediately at the back of

SHAKESPEARE'S THEATRE

The stage and its adjuncts; the tiring-house; and the auditorium.

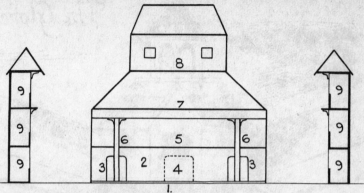

FIG I ELEVATION

1. Platform stage (approximately five feet above the ground) 2. Tiring-house
3. Tiring-house doors to stage 4. Conjectural third door 5. Tiring-house
gallery (balustrade and partitioning not shown) 6. Pillars supporting the
heavens 7. The heavens 8. The hut 9. The spectators' galleries

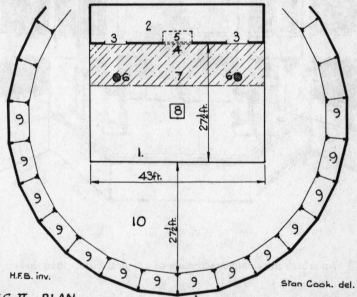

H.F.B. inv.   Stan Cook. del.

FIG II PLAN

1. Platform stage 2. Tiring-house 3. Tiring-house doors to stage
4. Conjectural third door 5. Conjectural discovery space (alternatively behind 3)
6. Pillars supporting the heavens 7. The heavens 8. Trap door 9. Spectators'
gallery 10. The yard

An artist's imaginative recreation of a typical Elizabethan theatre

the stage. The stage-direction 'within' means inside the tiring-house. Along its frontage, probably from the top of the second storey, juts out the canopy or 'Heavens', carried on two large pillars rising through the platform (6, 7) and sheltering the rear part of the stage, the rest of which, like the yard, was open to the sky. If the 'hut' (I.8), housing the machinery for descents, stood, as in the Swan drawing, above the 'Heavens', that covering must have had a trap-door, so that the descents could be made through it.

Descents are one illustration of the vertical dimension the dramatist could use to supplement the playing-area of the great platform. The other opportunities are provided by the tiring-house frontage or facade. About this facade the evidence is not as complete or clear as we should like, so that Fig. I is in part conjectural. Two doors giving entry to the platform there certainly were (3). A third (4) is probable but not certain. When curtained, a door, most probably this one, would furnish what must be termed a discovery-space (II.5), not an inner stage (on which action in any depth would have been out of sight for a significant part of the audience). Usually no more than two actors were revealed (exceptionally, three), who often then moved out on to the platform. An example of this is Ferdinand and Miranda in *The Tempest* 'discovered' at chess, then seen on the platform speaking with their fathers. Similarly the gallery (I.5) was not an upper stage. Its use was not limited to the actors: sometimes it functioned as 'lords' rooms' for favoured spectators, sometimes, perhaps, as a musicians' gallery. Frequently the whole gallery would not be needed for what took place aloft: a window-stage (as in the first balcony scene in *Romeo*, even perhaps in the second) would suffice. Most probably this would be a part (at one end) of the gallery itself; or just possibly, if the gallery did not (as it does in the Swan drawing) extend the whole width of the tiring-house, a window over the left or right-hand door. As the texts show, whatever was presented aloft, or in the discovery-space, was directly related to the action on the platform, so that at no time was there left, between the audience and the action of the drama, a great bare space of platform-stage. In relating Shakespeare's drama to the physical conditions of the theatre, the primacy of that platform is never to be forgotten.

Note: The present brief account owes most to C. Walter Hodges, *The Globe Restored*; Richard Hosley in *A New Companion to Shakespeare Studies*, and in *The Revels History of English Drama*; and to articles by Hosley and Richard Southern in *Shakespeare Survey*, 12, 1959, where full discussion can be found.

HAROLD BROOKS

FURTHER READING AND REFERENCES

Editions (with introductions and notes)
Jenkins, Harold (ed.), *Hamlet* (Arden Shakespeare, London: Methuen, 1982). Critical introduction, pp.122–59, text and commentary, and longer notes, pp.421–571.
Alexander, Nigel (ed.), *Hamlet* (London: Macmillan, 1973).
Spencer, T. J. B. (ed.), *Hamlet* (New Penguin, 1980) Introduction by Anne Barton.

Life and career
Schoenbaum, S., *William Shakespeare: A Compact Documentary Life* (Oxford: Clarendon Press, 1977).

Theatre and performance
Hodges, C. Walter, *Shakespeare's Theatre* (Oxford University Press, 1980).
Styan, J. L. *Shakespeare's Stagecraft* (Cambridge University Press, 1971).
Gilder, Rosamond, *John Gielgud's Hamlet* (London: Methuen, 1937).
Davison, Peter, *Hamlet* (Text and Performance series: London: Macmillan, 1983)
Styan, J. L., *Shakespeare's Stagecraft* (Cambridge University Press, 1971). *the Twentieth Century* (Cambridge University Press, 1977).

Criticism and close commentaries
Jump, John (ed.), *Shakespeare: Hamlet* (London: Macmillan Casebook, 1968).
Granville Barker, H., *Hamlet: Prefaces to Shakespeare*. III (London: Batsford, 1930).
Wilson, J. Dover, *What Happens in Hamlet* (Cambridge University Press, 1935).
Muir, Kenneth, *Shakespeare: Hamlet* (Studies in English Literature, London: Arnold, 1963).

Imagery
Clemen, W. H. *The Development of Shakespeare's Imagery*, Ch. 12 (London: Methuen, 1951).